About the Author

Cassandra Eason is an international author, broadcaster and psychic consultant. She has studied the history, psychology and esoteric practices of the Tarot for a number of years and has read the Tarot on numerous radio and television programmes throughout the world as well as lecturing on and teaching the subject to a variety of audiences. She has produced 18 books on the paranormal, magic and divination, spiritual and religious experience and is an expert on folklore and superstition.

Cassandra Eason offers occasional workshops in the Tarot and postal Tarot consultations. Contact Butterfly Promotions – Tel: 01709 830084; Fax: 01709 830883; Email: butterfly@mail.com – for further information.

Tarot

Piatkus Guides

Other titles in this series include

Celtic Wisdom
Crystal Wisdom
The Essential Nostradamus
Feng Shui
Meditation

A PIATKUS GUIDE

Tarot

Cassandra Eason

PIATKUS

© 1999 Cassandra Eason

First published in 1999 by
Judy Piatkus (Publishers) Ltd
5 Windmill Street, London W1P 1HF

The moral rights of the author have been asserted

A catalogue record for this book is available from the British Library

ISBN 0-7499-1872-1

Illustrations from the Universal Waite Tarot Deck reproduced by
permission of US Games Systems, Inc., Stamford, CT 06902, USA
Copyright © 1990 by US Games Systems, Inc.
Further reproduction prohibited

Set in 12.5/14 pt Perpetua
Typeset by Action Publishing Technology Limited, Gloucester
Printed & bound in Great Britain by
Mackays of Chatham PLC

Contents

Introduction

Tarot, a Mirror
for Your Soul

This book is a complete guide to learning the Tarot cards. The Tarot, with its universal symbolism and ability to link users directly with their own inner store of unconscious wisdom, can be used both as a tool of personal exploration and to give readings to other people.

From the first chapter you will use the cards for psychic readings for yourself and others. As you build up your knowledge and expertise, the readings will become gradually more complex so that by the end of the book you will be able to use the full pack and a variety of spreads or layouts. This book is intended both for the complete beginner and for more experienced Tarot readers who may want to return to the roots of the Tarot to consider alternative interpretations and to explore through the exercises the rich pictorial imagery as a focus for greater psychic awareness.

When I first encountered the Tarot cards nine years ago, frankly I was sceptical. Because of my somewhat rigid training in teaching and psychology, I tried to reduce them to an analytical tool. Deep down I was quite afraid. Although I was becoming an expert on the paranormal and had extensively researched the world of psychic children and psychic families, I still believed that I was entirely mistress of my fate and that the cards were only mirrors of what was already known, if not openly acknowledged. However, time and time again cards would appear in readings that exactly addressed the situation under question. Looking at the Tarot images I intuitively *knew* facts not available to me through rational deductive processes.

Over the last nine years I have given hundreds of Tarot readings in bookshops when publicising my writing, while teaching Tarot classes at the local education college, on radio and television, at lectures and more recently at workshops at health and healing exhibitions. I have written eighteen books on magic and divination that have moved further from the shores of logic and conscious knowledge and closer to intuition and unconscious wisdom. Although I have researched in detail and demonstrated more than forty different forms of divination, it is the Tarot that has proved the most potent and far-seeing method. It is an excellent basis for beginning psychic development.

To my growing surprise I discovered that the best readings I gave were those where I left behind the psychological and even historical basis of the Tarot and listened to the cards, letting the images create visual mirrors in my own psyche. The Tarot was startlingly accurate when I interacted with the person for whom I was reading and our intuitions met in the card layout. I realised too that what I had originally feared was opening my psyche to a wider awareness in which events do not just happen by chance. For the right cards do turn up time and time again and they can cast insight not only on the present, but on future possibilities and paths.

In this book I offer knowledge of the psychological and

historical background of the Tarot, but most importantly my own growing insights into the wisdom behind this spiritual and magical system. Ultimately, what you bring to the Tarot will determine how quickly you become expert. If you do follow your own innate intuitive abilities and trust the message the cards give to your heart and soul, you will rapidly become a sensitive and proficient Tarot reader.

This is the third book I have written on the Tarot and each time I cast off earlier preconceptions as I become aware of hidden meanings behind specific cards. For Tarot knowledge grows and evolves and the key to successful Tarot reading, whether for yourself, for friends or eventually professionally, lies in practice and in constantly re-assessing your knowledge in the light of experience.

How to Use the Book

Each chapter offers a new skill, whether a group of related cards to learn or a new spread and exercises to explore different aspects of the Tarot. The format is one I have used successfully for teaching many times.

You can read the whole book first or work stage by stage through it, doing the exercises and trying out the spreads.

There are various stages at which you can pause for a while or even stop, for example after you have learned the Major Arcana, the first 22 cards and a basic nine-card spread. Some readers do profound readings with just the Major Arcana and a basic layout. However, you may develop all the skills in this book and then wish to read more about the background of the Tarot. I have listed some useful books for this purpose in the Further Reading section.

I have also suggested keeping a Tarot diary of your own personal readings and to record your findings in the exercises.

Like any journal you can look back and see how far you have travelled and in time, if you decide to teach others the Tarot or write about it, you have a valuable personal source book.

What is the Tarot?

The Tarot pack comprises 78 highly illustrated cards that seem to have originated in medieval Europe. Today they are associated mainly with magic and divination, but for a long time they were used for card games. The first 22 cards, which can vary slightly in order and name depending on the type of pack, are called the Major Arcana (Arcana means hidden secrets) and are based on symbols that have had meaning since the beginning of civilisation. Some people use only these Major cards in readings and they can be valuable indicators of life changes and our inner world.

The Minor Arcana includes 40 numbered cards from Ace (or one) to ten in each of four suits. *Cups* or chalices; *Pentacles*, coins or discs; *Wands* or staves; and *Swords* correspond with the four traditional playing card suits: Hearts, Diamonds, Clubs and Spades. But the Tarot suits also represent what the ancients regarded as the basic elements: *Water, Earth, Fire* and *Air*, and the spiritual qualities associated with these elements. In a reading, these number cards tend to refer to specific issues and courses of action.

There are also the 16 Court cards – four more than the usual playing card deck. The jack takes on two aspects: the Page and the Knight (sometimes the Page is regarded as the feminine side of youthfulness). The court cards can have different names such as Princess and Prince, Daughter and Son, or even Priestesses and Shamans instead of the traditional Queens and Kings, but most keep the traditional titles. These court cards usually refer to personalities or aspects of personalities and, as such, are excellent for dealing with relationship issues.

The Origins and Symbolism

We cannot trace the history of the Tarot definitively, though attempts have been made to link it with early gypsy tribes, to the Kaballa (the Jewish lore) and to alchemists, or to define it as a vehicle for concealing the esoteric wisdom of persecuted religious sects. The fact that so many traditions have an affinity to the Tarot demonstrates that it can be used to express many belief systems and cultural backgrounds. The concepts behind any valid divinatory system are central to the human condition. They are all in the Tarot: mother, father, the divine child, the wise man, the virgin, the hero, the lover and the trickster, as well as more traditional virtues of endurance, patience, moderation and justice.

Tarot cards seem to be a mediaeval creation, although the images and themes are much older. The Bibliothèque Nationale in Paris has seventeen ornate cards, sixteen of them Tarot Trumps, originally believed to have been made for Charles VI of France around 1392, but now thought to be Italian, dating from about 1470.

One suggestion is that Tarot cards sprang from the north of Italy, in the valley of the Taro River, which is a tributary of the River Po. This could have influenced the Italian name for the cards, *Tarrochi*, and the French name, *Tarot*. The modern Tarot pack comes directly from an Italian version, the Venetian or Piedmontese Tarot, which has 22 Trumps. The same form is found in the French pack called the Tarot of Marseilles, which is still popular. Both designs were in popular use by about 1500 in Northern Italy and France.

The four suits represented different strata of society: the

swords as the aristocracy, cups or chalices as the clergy and monastic orders, coins for the merchant and batons for the peasants.

Another theory claimed that the gypsies brought the Tarot with them in their long trek to Europe from India via the Middle East. In 1781, a time when Egypt was seen as the source of all knowledge, Antoine Court de Gebelin, a French Protestant clergyman who became fascinated by the occult, found some friends playing with Tarot cards. He identified the cards as containing the secrets of the priests of Ancient Egypt, hidden in the symbols to protect this wisdom from invading barbarians. The Arabic word *Tariqua* ('the way of wisdom') bears some resemblance to Tarot and the Ancient Egyptian word *Tarosh* means the Royal Way.

The greatest influence on modern Tarot readings is Arthur Edward Waite, who in 1891 joined the Order of the Golden Dawn, a mystical group whose members included the poet W.B. Yeats. The Tarot was important to the Golden Dawn, which traced its traditions back to the mysterious Rosicrucians of the seventeenth century. They in turn drew on alchemical and Kabbalistic traditions dating back to the time of Moses. The Rider Waite Tarot pack, with its illustrated Minor Arcana, was intended to promote visions as well as to be used for divination. Waite associated the four suits with the four sacred objects of the Holy Grail quest – the cup and the plate used at the Last Supper, the lance and the sword. Many of his cards reflect the romantic Arthurian background of the Grail legends.

The darker associations of the Tarot came from the occultist Aleister Crowley, who broke away from the Order of the Golden Dawn. Crowley believed he was the reincarnation of Eliphas Levi and added sexual and negative connotations to magic and the Tarot. This has done the cards and their spiritual symbolism a great disservice and out of all the countless positive associations sadly this is the aspect that is too frequently remembered.

Choosing a Tarot Pack

This book is illustrated with the Universal Waite Tarot Pack as it is probably one of the most widely available packs and has the benefit of a highly illustrated Minor Arcana whose meanings have been borrowed by creators of Tarot packs and readers everywhere. But the book is not linked to any specific system and you can use absolutely any pack that corresponds to the order and symbolism of the core Tarot suits.

Eventually you may buy several packs because at different times each addresses a special need (see section on suggested card packs on p. 137).

How Does the Tarot Work?

Some people believe an external power controls their apparently random choice, either a spirit guide or that of the person who is reading for them. I believe we are primarily using internal powers of intuition and inspiration. The psychologist Carl Jung believed that our collective unconscious gives us access to the experiences and accumulated wisdom of mankind. This level of experience enables us to move beyond the present and past to glimpse not a fixed future, but possibilities and choices just over the horizon. Some kind of telepathic power influences our apparently random selection of cards, perhaps akin to telekinesis where the mind can influence inanimate objects, so that they are relevant to issues we hadn't even consciously realised were troubling us.

Tarot Rituals

When you first buy your Tarot pack, there are very simple rituals that can offer both psychic protection and energise your artefacts. These are based on the ancient elements Earth, Air, Fire and Water which were regarded once as the composition of all life and are still symbols of the qualities of sensation, thought, intuition and feeling that together make up the integrated world view of Jungian psychology.

☆ Place your Tarot pack in a circle, either drawn clockwise on paper or created from a necklace. The circle contains and amplifies natural energies.

☆ Pass over your cards first a dish of salt for the grounding power and protection of Earth. As you do so visualise magic standing stones and ancient circles, tall jagged rocks, mountains, vast sandy plains.

☆ Move next above it a lighted incense stick of pine or rosemary for energy and clarity of thought, or sandalwood for psychic power and healing powers. This will endow your cards with the keen perceptions and searching insights of Air.

☆ For the inspiration and creativity of Fire, light a golden, yellow or red candle and raise this above the cards.

☆ Finally, pass a dish of Water steeped with rose petals, or rose or lavender essential oil, for harmony and sensitivity to the deeper emotions of those for whom you may read.

☆ Leave the circle and cards objects on a window sill for a sun and moon cycle of twenty-four hours, then return them, wrapped if you wish in dark silk, to the box.

Keep your Tarot cards wrapped in dark silk in a drawer or box when you are not using them. I used to laugh at ritual, but gradually have learned that it is important to make a sacred space for this important part of your life.

Psychic Protection and Divination

If you avoid carrying out divination or psychic work when you are feeling exhausted or negative, your explorations should be entirely harmonious and positive. Because you do become very sensitive to atmospheres the more you evolve psychically, it is important to establish a psychic space in which to work and to close down this area after you have finished so that you are not awake all night.

Even in a public place, before giving a reading you can use your mind's eye to draw around yourself a clockwise circle, beginning in the north, that encloses you in golden light. When you have finished giving a reading, close down the circle in an anti-clockwise direction beginning again in the north by visual-ising a dark crystal such as a smoky quartz or obsidian overwriting the golden light and leaving you at peace.

If you are reading for someone else, mentally enclose them in a separate circle of protection, so that if they do have negative vibes through sadness or anxiety these are dispelled at the end of the reading.

For extra protection, you can place crystals either in the corner of the room or the four corners of the table where you are working, or on the table or floor directly in front of you whenever you give a reading, to act as a psychic shield from any negativity – intended or unintended. Protective crystals include black agate, amethysts, bloodstones, carnelians, garnets, black and red jasper, lapis lazuli, tiger's eye, topaz and turquoise.

If you have read for someone else, pass your crystal pendulum or an amethyst over your cards in an anti-clockwise direction to draw any negative feelings. Wash the pendulum and crystal under running water, afterwards resting it in black silk for a while. In my book, *The Complete Guide to Psychic Development* (see Further Reading section) are more detailed examples of psychic protection.

Reading for Yourself

The very best readings you do will always be for yourself.

For me, the Tarot is still primarily a personal guide. It's certainly not unlucky to read for yourself. In time you will be able to read anywhere. But at first make your own readings a special occasion in your life, making time to be quiet and uninterrupted. You may like to take a scented bath first and wear something loose and be warm and perhaps light a candle and have your crystals near you. But equally if you can't be alone for long and end up wearing your old jeans, crammed in the kitchen while the television or stereo from next door blares through your consciousness, you can still get excellent readings. The magic is within you and makes no demands or conditions except a willingness to listen to your inner voice.

Can You Use the Tarot to Foretell the Future?

Unless you believe that the future is fixed and we are all running along a pre-ordained track like so many mechanical toys, neither the Tarot nor any other divinatory tool can say what will definitely happen six or twelve months from now.

What the Tarot can do is to enable us to scan the horizon

and spy far-off potential dangers or opportunities and react to them. We can step momentarily outside linear time and see the change points ahead. By anticipating alternative possibilities, we can make choices and help others to shape the future in the most positive way possible.

On the other hand, we may decide that deep down we don't want to go for the changes on offer and we'll enjoy life in the slow lane with time to watch the flowers grow. The Tarot can sometimes surprise us by revealing the opposite of what we consciously say or do, and yet that may be the solution that was waiting to be discovered. Fortune-making is much more satisfying than fortune-telling.

EXERCISE 1: Beginning to Use Your Tarot

The Tarot is an aid to developing your intuition. The best reading is probably this first one you do before you know the set meanings, for your natural intuition and links with the collective wisdom or mankind will guide you to the right meanings.

☆ Read for a friend or family member who knows nothing of the Tarot, to avoid his or her preconceptions.

☆ Shuffle or mix the whole pack and then get the person for whom you are reading to do the same, while thinking of a specific question or issue, so that your psychic vibrations join together.

☆ If the questioner wishes, let him or her divide the pack into three and then take six cards from one of the piles without looking at the cards.

☆ Let the questioner spread the cards facing him or her, in two rows of three, beginning at the left and moving to the right and then from right to left with the second row.

☆ Turn the cards over one at a time, beginning with the first placed.

☆ When the six are face upwards, see if you get a general impression. If so, trust this pure intuition. Even experienced readers rely on this first glimpse as the truest picture.

☆ See next whether there are any of the Major name cards that seem to relate to a specific person or situation and do the same with the Court cards, the Kings, Queens, Knights and Pages.

☆ Look at the number cards. Does one suit predominate and if so what does this suggest intuitively?

☆ Try to create a story from the cards and you will find that what you say – if you speak from the heart and psyche – will have reached the heart of the matter.

☆ Do not forget to ask the questioner for any meanings that seem relevant. The best readings are always a dialogue.

☆ Either tape-record or scribble down your results. You will be amazed when you learn the card meanings how accurate you were.

Reversed Cards

This book does not contain references to reversed cards because these are often merely the result of the way a pack is shuffled or dealt. There is no psychic significance. Each card contains within itself both a positive and a negative aspect and how these manifest in a reading will depend on the meaning of the whole reading and also on how the reader and the subject interpret that card on an intuitive level.

1

First Steps in Tarot Reading

The Major Arcana cards in the Tarot pack fall naturally into themes that reflect a person's journey through life to greater awareness. The Tarot story begins in the unformed self, the hope and innocence in the Fool. It ends in experience in the card of the World, where actions are based on wisdom and awareness yet the youthful optimism of the first card still shines through.

The Cards of Your Inner Powers

These are the cards that deal with the real essential person in us all, the separate identity we have, the unique talents and the way we learn to adapt this core self to the demands of the external world. They will always be key cards, appearing in a reading when identity is under question or the issue is one central to happiness.

The Fool is the first of the 22 cards of the Major Arcana and he is far from foolish. Like the Joker in card games, he can do anything or be anyone and change the whole course of the game at a stroke. In literature, he's the Fool of Shakespeare's *King Lear* who is not afraid to speak the truth though he may suffer for it. He's Jung's inner child, the essential self stripped of worldly trappings, the real person that integrates our competitive and caring sides. In alchemy, he is the divine hermaphrodite, the offspring of the marriage of King Sol and Queen Luna.

In the Universal Waite Tarot Pack, he is accompanied by his dog, perhaps representing the instinctive ability to find the right track. He is travelling light and about to leap off a precipice – not a leap into the dark but a leap into the light. You can read many different interpretations of the card or any other Fool card you may use but the art is not in saying, 'He's holding the white rose, an alchemical symbol for rebirth,' but in interpreting what the Fool is saying in your life and in each individual reading.

The Fool is for me the most important card in the pack because he is saying: 'Trust your own wisdom.' You already have the power of the Fool within you and with it the key not only to the Tarot but to making your own fortune. But to rely on this intuition when the facts may suggest otherwise is very much a leap into the dark and sometimes it means leaving the safe option. This is the negative aspect of following your intuition because sometimes it does mean giving up the security that keeps many of us tied in less than satisfactory situations. You may even end up hurting people who can't understand why we've got to rock the boat or leave them behind. So we must be aware that it can be a lonely road with no going back and there may be regrets you'll have to come to terms with later.

The Fool is a very exciting card. It indicates there's a decision to be made and no clear pointers as to the right answer. Ignore all the good advice you've been given about acting with caution and follow your gut feeling. Don't agonise, but trust yourself.

The Magician is the card of creative energies. He's the archetypal trickster who holds the key to enlightenment. Some associate him with the winged Mercury, god of travel, communication, health, commerce – and thieves. He can also be slightly frightening because the world of magic always carries with it the unknown element. We all have magic within us but it's up to us whether we use our powers, earthly or magical, for good or ill.

The Magician is the creative energy needed to put your plans into action. When it appears, you need to use every resource you've got and a few you've borrowed to start that new project. It's time to learn new skills for changes at work or even to make the most of your leisure. The Magician is the card of 'now'. Something is bubbling up inside and you feel excited and eager for change. Even if you feel exhausted, take advantage of that small spark inside and let the energy build up.

But beware. The Magician can cut ethical corners, with his or her eye on the main chance. When you see others flouting rules and regulations, the Magician whispers, 'Why not you too?' But remember, you need to succeed in a way that you can be open about and not be ashamed of.

The High Priestess or ***Popess*** gets her name from the legendary ninth-century Pope Joan but is also very much associated with the maiden and the virgin goddesses such as the waxing moon Greek goddess Artemis or the Celtic Brigid, patroness of healers and poets. In some packs she is called Juno, wife of the supreme Roman god Jupiter, in her sense as the abstract, wise feminine principle of divinity rather than the sensual Mother Goddess.

This card can apply equally to men and women for this is a card of the inner world, inner change and aloneness (not necessarily loneliness). The High Priestess is 'the separate you', the unchanging person you've been in essence from a child and will be when you're ninety. It's about the real you, not you as loyal partner, supportive friend, team member, son, daughter or parent. The power of the *High Priestess* lies in his or her acceptance that, much as you love others and need approval, you can be happy in your own company.

The High Priestess is a reminder of your own priorities and searchings for meaning. Finding the High Priestess buried in yourself is identifying that real you. It is time to start thinking about what it is that makes you, not other people, happy. Take, demand or steal time every day, even a few minutes to be by yourself.

The High Priestess is the other side of the Empress, giving and nurturing and empathising with others, and both are a vital ingredient in our make-up whether man or woman. The former's negative aspect is a tendency to be a cold fish, so aware of her own identity that she fails to understand and tolerate the weaknesses and needs of others.

The Cards of Responsibility to Others

These cards concern the way the inner self is modified by the influence of key people in our lives, from parents and authority figures to those inner controls that act as a brake on irresponsibility, but can also keep redundant warnings and prohibitions in our heads. They may appear in readings when the influence of others is weighing heavily.

The Empress is the Mother Earth card and easily recognised as a lady from whom all manner of goodies flow. She represents the Mother Goddess and earth mother typified by Ceres or Demeter, the corn goddess of the classics, Cerridwen of the Celts, goddess of the full moon, or Frigg in the Norse legends, goddess of women and mothers and the Northern housewife.

The aspects of the Empress are not restricted to mothers or even women, although even today women take on much of the practical caring for families and elderly. We still often equate male caring with providing material security and some women do feel threatened when a man cares for a baby or applies for a job as a midwife or au pair. So when I talk of 'she', it's because the card depicts a woman, though if we think of it as a receptive card then it's nearer the truth.

Who is the Empress? You of course: the nurturer, nurse, lover, provider, soother of battered egos and refuge for every lame duck who comes quacking at your door. And why not? Loving and caring is central to human nature though, as I've said, it can be harder even today for men to display this vital quality. We aren't aiming to get rid of the Empress, only to give the High Priestess a look in as well. So long as the giving doesn't go too far, it is a creative and important side of you. The High Priestess aspect on her own can be a bit of a cold fish.

If you get the Empress in a reading, you can be sure that your emotional or practical support are vital to those around you and whether with your family, friends or even work life your role is making a happy environment. You know that people are more important than things and that usually compromise is better than confrontation. Yet there is a negative side to the Empress. What starts out as giving can end as exploitation, so that you feel you've lost sight of your own needs and identity. It's all a question of balance. Whether at home or work you can begin to say no to at least some of the demands if you are starting to feel resentful or just plain frazzled. Just a thought – are you the one always offering your help because you are afraid of being thought badly of if you don't keep proving how indispensable you are?

 The Emperor is the creative card. He represents the competitive logical assertive side of us that, man or woman, we need to survive. As the Empress is the Mother Goddess, the Emperor is the All-Father of many traditions: Zeus in classical mythology, the Norse Odin the Wise One or Woden in the Anglo-Saxon tradition. He is pictured enthroned, often in battle dress, for he is the experienced warrior as well as leader of his people. But, although he is the giver of law and decisions, laws may not always be just and decisions are not always wise.

Just as some men find it hard to express their Empress side, it is still very hard for women to be assertive and competitive. Tradition still emphasises that girls should be nice and polite and both men and women are left with very conflicting messages in what can be a dog-eat-dog society.

The Emperor warns that it may be time for you to assert what you want and be prepared to go for it, whether it is a career move, a desire to change your house or lifestyle. You may have been hesitating because it involves a confrontation, but be brave and act now.

The Emperor is so positive that he is bound to have a strongly negative aspect. He is particularly hard to please, not a very welcoming character no matter which Tarot pack you use. Most of us have an Emperor in our lives. He is not necessarily a man. It could be your mother, your mother-in-law, a tutor at college, your boss, even a 'friendly' neighbour or your best friend who is digging under the foundations of your confidence, always pointing out your mistakes 'for your own good' and putting you right.

 The Hierophant or *Pope* represents the conventional path to wisdom or success. However brilliant your inspirations and intuitions, there comes a time to pay attention to detail – the computer manual has to be read, the examination questions studied and the brown envelopes opened. So the Hierophant may not exactly excite you unless you enjoy sitting in libraries or poring over accounts, but he's very necessary. In the classics he is Saturn or the Saxon's Seater, the god of limitation and fate. In some packs he is called Jupiter, the Roman name for Zeus. He mirrors the Emperor, but in wisdom and knowledge rather than authority.

The Hierophant indicates that you've got to use a conventional approach, whether it's seeking professional advice or paying attention to the small print. But that's not necessarily bad news because often, once you've got the necessary knowledge or training, or even sorted out all those unpaid bills, you can get a real sense of achievement.

While the Magician whispers 'Let's cut corners', the Hierophant insists we take each painstaking step. Perhaps you've been offered a bit of excitement or happiness, but you know it's at the expense of others and so it's not for you.

But the Hierophant has a negative side. His conservatism can cause guilty feelings. He's the brother of the less positive side of the Emperor, dedicated to keeping you in your place and making you feel guilty about your shortcomings. He's your conscience when you contemplate any misdeeds.

A THREE-CARD READING BASED ON THE FIRST SIX CARDS

Since all the cards represent facets of ourselves, you can answer simple questions or make decisions by shuffling the first six cards of the Major Arcana, picking three at random and laying them face down left to right. Turn all three over and see what initial impression you receive before looking at the individual cards. Build them up into a story.

I gave the following reading to Trisha, a divorcee in her thirties with no children, who had been offered a university place to read Egyptology, her passion. Her friends and family told her she was mad to give up a highly paid job and a nice flat to move a hundred miles away and struggle on a grant for a qualification that would not even guarantee her a career. The three cards she selected were the Fool, the High Priestess and the Magician.

THE FOOL.   THE HIGH PRIESTESS   THE MAGICIAN.

Trisha, who had never had a Tarot reading before, commented that cards did not seem to be advising her to play safe. The Fool represented a step into the unknown, the Magician a time to learn new skills and reawaken a creative spark that perhaps got lost over the last few years in her work.

The High Priestess was the real essential Trisha who loved going off alone to pore over Egyptian artefacts in the British Museum, to holiday alone in Egypt and study hieroglyphics hour after hour, rather than the supportive friend, loving daughter and efficient businesswoman, the persona she portrayed to the world. Trisha said that the reading told her what she knew deep in her heart, that ultimately she would regret it if she did not take this opportunity. A gamble, but that is what the Fool is all about – and we may already deep down have started on a path in our dreams that with courage we could fulfil in reality.

EXERCISE 2: Choosing a Card of the Day

Many traditional spreads rely on choosing a card, called the Signifier, to represent you, sometimes in the first position of a reading. Often it is suggested that you choose a Court card either for yourself or someone else to represent their appearance. For example, the King of Wands usually stands for a mature man over 35 who has brown hair and a fairish skin. Few of us divide people like that in real life. The colour of your hair and skin has little to do with the way you are. And, as for maturity, age is not always the defining factor. Rather than choosing a significant card for a reading, let your intuition select a single card each morning as your guide. One card may take on special importance and appear at regular intervals for days, weeks or months.

Liz, a single parent stuck in a job she hated in order to provide for her children, got Strength (the card of sticking at a situation) at least three times a week as her first card. Then she started to get the Fool (the leap into the unknown) as her first card and Strength disappeared. This rattled her so much that she checked several times to make sure that Strength was still in the pack.

On the third morning that the Fool appeared Liz saw an advert for a live-in job running an animal sanctuary up north and applied on impulse. She loved animals and already had a house full of strays. The card continued to appear every couple of days and before long she'd got the job and moved house. She now gets the Empress (Mother Earth) card frequently and is blissfully happy dating a nature reserve warden.

2

Exploring the
Major Arcana

The next six cards move away from inner exploration to encountering and resolving relationship issues, questions of fate and destiny. They often appear when external events are exerting a powerful control over the life path.

The Cards of Everyday Living

In a sense these cards encompass the movement from inner exploration to encountering and resolving relationship issues, questions of fate and destiny.

 The Lovers, the card of Relationships, features the romantic, scantily clad Adam and Eve in the Garden of Eden before the serpent told them about good and evil. The Lovers are rooted firmly in relationships, not only sexual love but also platonic love. Questions involving relationships are one of the main reasons people consult the Tarot. Of course, some of the questions can lead us up a blind alley, the most common being: 'Will I meet Mr/Ms Right?' The correct question is perhaps: 'How can I avoid ending up with another Mr/Ms Wrong after a disastrous relationship or maybe a whole series of them?' Or 'Should I settle for Mr/Ms Nearly Right or hang on in hope?'

In the real world, the Lovers is not about wine and roses, but your dealings with those nearest, if not dearest to you. These may be boyfriend, partner, parents, kids or all the other relatives and close friends.

The Lovers may appear because these close relationships have been filling your thoughts recently. Do you feel discouraged by the media image of families, comparing the perfection of TV adverts with your own less harmonious existence? Or, if you are still single, do you wonder where the romance and love are?

The card may be promising new love or that a new relationship will blossom. However, it may equally suggest now might be a good time to further relationships, whether with the guy in the office who's maybe a foot shorter than you'd envisaged your dream partner, or the girl who is definitely the before in the diet advert but always asks after your weekend and your elderly grandmother. Or perhaps it's time to rediscover the person you are married to. There are questions about a relationship and maybe a few choices to be made when the Lovers appears, but for once the grass might actually be greener on your own side of your fence.

As for the negative side of the Lovers: sometimes we lock ourselves into roles, based on some false ideal of family happiness — good mother, daddy's little girl, the loyal son, the protective father — that no longer apply. In this way we hold on to relationships that have run their course.

The Chariot is the card of change and ultimately triumph, of 'choosing the route' and changing to the direction you want. It's no easy business, moving away from the familiar world and maybe balancing conflicting elements. It's vital that you choose the direction so you can't complain about the destination. And that's what the Chariot is about: using your own impetus to get moving. Whether black and white horses or sphinxes pull the chariot, the card indicates that the rider has harnessed opposing powers to give the impetus to succeed. When you are young, the pressures to fit in with the crowd or live up to parental expectations can be very strong. You can end up doing what other people decided was best in your career and even in choosing a partner. Older people too can encounter pressure if they suddenly want to change course: grown-up children can be the worst tyrants of all, wanting to preserve the status quo for mum and dad.

The Chariot indicates that the winds of change have been blowing and you are being carried in a direction you don't like. Maybe you don't want to go to college but all the forms are signed and your parents have bought you a set of matching suitcases; or your partner is moving to the other end of the country and assumes you will follow; or the kids may be about to leave home and you are wondering what to do with your life; or perhaps the job you can do with your eyes shut is suddenly less certain.

The negative aspect of the Chariot involves constantly changing the external circumstances when it's an inner problem; changing jobs at the first setback; not sticking with relationships if the going gets tough; constantly having new friends and new interests but finding that your enthusiasm cools rapidly. We've got to be sure we are changing the right things and not just moving the old play to a new theatre with a different cast.

 Justice is not purely a card of litigation. It talks of an important principle that you see as central to your happiness, whether it's a fairer working environment or a more equal division of labour at home, among flatmates or family. It is a very positive card whether you are fighting petty injustice or a big issue.

Justice is not the most approachable card in the pack: a stern-faced creature balancing the scales as she sits on top of the Old Bailey dispensing wise words on monumental issues. But although the Justice card can refer to legal and official matters, its most usual meaning is in connection with any compromises you are being asked to make in your life. If the issue is a core one, Justice says that you should not be persuaded or coerced into abandoning your principles.

The negative side of Justice is a tendency to repress minor niggles to keep the peace. This can build up resentment. Whether it's a flatmate who constantly borrows your belongings without asking, or your best friend who always assumes you'll pay for joint outings because you earn more, or a family member who complains you've bought the wrong flavour yoghurt, unresolved unfairness can build up till you explode at entirely the wrong person or time.

If this is the case, try identifying specific areas however seemingly petty where you are being unfairly treated and say, 'Well actually I do mind' or even 'No'.

The Cards of Reacting to Fate

We can't always head off misfortune or guarantee good luck. What we can do is affect what ultimately happens by reacting to events or flowing with them rather than fighting the current.

 The Hermit is the card of our inner voice and wisdom for he represents the archetypal wise man. For some, this may involve occult knowledge or formal spiritual paths. But for the majority of us it is a far more personal process of awareness. Ultimately the path of the Hermit is a lonely one.

THE HERMIT.

The Hermit may be a pointer that it's time to step back from the world and from the demands of others and give yourself time. Often the Hermit will appear if someone is acting as a peacemaker for other people's quarrels, whether in the family or at work, and getting complaints from both sides. It can be exhausting to stand between warring combatants and ultimately enable those involved to opt out of the responsibility for resolving their differences.

The negative side of the Hermit is over-reliance on the wisdom of others, whether an expert in health, education, psychology or science, or on a personal level an older person who offers guidance. If the card appears with the Emperor, this may be because we move from one authority figure to another seeking perhaps the love and approval we were denied as children.

While we can learn a great deal from others – whether the accumulated wisdom of ages or from an experienced colleague or relation – ultimately we've got to assess that wisdom and listen to our own inner voice. We do have within ourselves the resources to answer our own questions, though we may not always like the answers.

The Wheel of Fortune is the card of finding the best solution in the face of unexpected change. It varies in different packs, depending on who is turning the Wheel. It may be the blindfolded goddess Fortuna, suggesting that man is subject to the whims of fate. Other packs show the Egyptian jackal-headed god Anubis, conductor of dead souls, or the Egyptian god Amon, controller of destiny and life. In the Buddhist philosophy the Wheel of Birth, Death and Rebirth is turned by man's own actions in different incarnations, so this symbol contains the element of choice and responsibility. This card never predicts that either good or bad fortune will strike, but usually refers to either a fear of disaster, hope of fortune, or some twist of fate.

Unexpected events – the job loss or move, the unplanned pregnancy, an illness, even a win on the lottery – can make you feel as if life is suddenly beyond your control. Sometimes we've contributed to that apparent bolt out of the blue: for example, by not answering the letters from the taxman or stuffing the bills we can't pay in a drawer and pretending they never came.

Whatever the rights or wrongs, the important thing is how we respond. Whether we react aggressively, pretend it isn't happening, or actually face it, we maximise or minimise the consequences. You may not have the power entirely to choose your course of action but there is always some room for manoeuvre, even in the most seemingly inflexible situations, and the smallest reaction may be crucial. If in doubt, it may be time to imitate the Hermit and withdraw until you feel able to make a decision or have the confidence to follow your intuition.

The negative side of the Wheel of Fortune comes when you allow others to impose a fixed vision of the future. If

29

you think of the Wheel as a ship's wheel then you need constantly to respond to circumstance either with evasive action or by holding straight until the tempest passes.

Strength, sometimes called Force or Fortitude, shows a woman closing or opening the mouth of a lion or Heracles wrestling with a lion. The woman is sometimes seen as the anima, the female magician, and in some packs has a magician's hat but not his wand, showing that a personal, gentler approach can be more effective than brute aggression. Strength talks of life as it is, sometimes mundane or hard, and shows that by weathering out a situation, whether a rocky patch in a relationship or an apparently unrecognised period of effort at work, you can win through.

Strength may appear when you have been considering giving up when you are on a slow path to achievement and others overtake, seemingly without any effort. But you will get there in the end if you keep going. And if you do use persuasion and are prepared to compromise then you will get what you want.

What is the negative side of Strength? Sticking in a no-win situation because you feel you aren't strong enough to walk away, pouring energy and time into someone or something that can never come good, hoping against hope to get someone else to change. You'll know when this is the case – that's the easy bit. The hard bit is cutting your losses and accepting that it really is time to use your strength for yourself.

EXERCISE 3: A Six-card Spread

Try a six-card spread based on the first 12 cards. Shuffle and deal face down six cards in two rows of three, from left to right for Row 1, and Row 2 right to left. Turn over your cards one at a time and see if you can get an overall impression before looking at the individual cards. See if any naturally fit together, for example the Emperor and Empress, and whether you immediately associate them with any individuals in your life.

The best way to learn is from other people's readings. Frank is in his fifties and has been at his present level at work for some years while younger people are overtaking him. Now the firm has been taken over by a multinational. He has been offered a chance to retrain although colleagues say he'd do better to ask for redundancy now rather than being edged out if he fails. Frank is afraid he's too old to learn new tricks but knows he probably won't get another job at his age (see next page).

Frank picks Strength as his key or first card, the Wheel of Fortune as his second, the Hermit as his third, the Hierophant as his fourth, the Emperor as his fifth and the Magician as his sixth.

Strength is clearly telling Frank to stick to his guns and not be deterred by the successful youngsters. He should ignore their comments that may hide their own fears. His experience and perseverance haven't brought results so far, but it's worth giving the new situation a try.

The Wheel of Fortune reflects the potential turmoil of the takeover. Whether or not this benefits Frank will depend on his reaction to the shake-up and the opportunity to move into a new field. It could even be seen as good fortune in getting Frank out of a rut.

The Hermit tells Frank to listen to himself and not his sniping colleagues and to keep out of office politics. He's apprehensive enough without all the doubters putting in their negative feelings. It also reminds him of all his inner resources.

The Hierophant encourages Frank to take the conventional path, the training course, and to put in effort to mastering the new skills that will give him a chance to succeed and maybe overtake his colleagues.

This is emphasised by the ambition and the drive of the Emperor, which reminds Frank that he has succeeded in the past and can do so again. It is very easy to go along with the negative perceptions of others and Frank has been shunted into the slow track which would be fine if that was where he wanted to be. The new management obviously considers he's worth retraining.

Finally, the Magician confirms the creative energy at Frank's disposal but says he has to translate plans into action now and not live on past successes or dreams.

EXERCISE 4: Continuing Your Tarot Diary

Keep recording your Tarot of the day and any readings you may make for yourself or others. Now you know more cards, your daily card is increasingly representative, so if you do keep getting the same card, ask yourself why. For example, if you get the Empress for several days, you may be doing too much for others and perhaps feeling resentful.

If a card appears a great deal, meditate on it or even sleep with it under your pillow. Insight may come, even in a dream.

Study your diary and see whether patterns emerge according to certain situations. For example, on the morning you are due to visit a relation who often criticises you, does the Hierophant inevitably appear as your card of the day? Are you absorbing unnecessary criticism from your relation or do you still feel obliged to take advice on situations of which he or she may have little knowledge because the person guided you wisely in childhood?

If you find that your Tarot diary is pointing to a card and you cannot see a solution or do not fully understand, use it as the basis for a fuller reading. Take the key card, for example the Hierophant, and place it as your first card in a reading. Add five more cards picked face down from a shuffled pack at random and see what the reading is saying about your underlying feelings and a possible solution.

On the other hand, a card may appear to encourage you to persist on a course, for example Strength or Justice, when other people are trying to dissuade you. If in doubt, pick a second card of the day and see what extra information it holds.

3

Using the Full Major Arcana for Readings

The later cards in the Major Arcana mirror the need to reconcile yourself with the world as it is with inevitable endings and losses without which there can be no gain. From this acceptance comes freedom, mature happiness and a new awareness based on what is possible. Many people, as they come to use the Major Arcana, can identify both situations and periods of their life with the cards and their steady progression towards understanding.

The Cards of Reality

The next three Tarot cards are the cards of reality, the world that is, not the world of our dreams. They are important cards if we are to move forward in a realistic way rather than dreaming or regretting our life away. They look at loss, at endings that must be faced if there are to be new beginnings and the sacrifice of immediate gratification for long-term gain in spiritual as well as material terms.

The Hanged Man, the card of sacrifice for greater advantage, is often represented by the Norse god Odin, the All-Father who hung by his feet from the world tree, Ygdrassil, for nine days and nights in search of enlightenment. Odin finally saw the runes beneath him and in reaching down for them found he was free. So letting go is perhaps a better way of thinking about of the Hanged Man. It's not an intuitive leap like the Fool's but a deliberate decision based on experience and maybe disillusion. Like Odin we may discover sometimes the answer isn't in relentless progress but by going back to what really matters, even giving up security or an easy lifestyle for what is important to us.

The Hanged Man is a positive, exciting card. It may appear when you've come to a crossroads and must decide whether to cut back now to save for the future, or even take on extra commitments and cut down on your leisure or sleep for a better job, or even to combine work and a family. Or you're contemplating a pay cut to do something you think is worthwhile. We all have our own Hanged Man scenarios but the underlying concept is the same.

What is the negative side of the Hanged Man? You can become addicted to sacrifice, even for the best of motives. Nothing is sadder than an elderly, embittered parent who rounds on his or her children and says, 'I gave up everything for you and now I have nothing.' So too, if you are caring for an elderly relative or even making compromises in your own lifestyle for a partner.

Death, the card of natural change, is the card with the most evil, yet undeserved, reputation: THERE IS ABSOLUTELY NO WAY THAT TURNING UP THE DEATH CARD MEANS THAT YOU, OR ANYONE CLOSE TO YOU, IS GOING TO DIE. Death is merely a reflection of an inner state that already exists but which you may be ignoring or resisting. As such its positive meaning far outweighs any negative connotations.

Death is sometimes portrayed as the mediaeval Grim Reaper with a scythe, as a black skeleton, or as a knight in black armour with a skull revealed through the helmet. Death comes to us all, but equally inevitable is change and the 'death' of a stage in our life. If we can face change with the same calm courage and optimism as a child, change can be positive. Death indicates that a natural change is already taking place, one which you might not yet be aware of or perhaps are trying to hold back. But it is time to move on, to cast aside childish things and to grow, however painful that process.

There are bound to be regrets whether the change involves leaving home for the first time, making a permanent commitment, having a family, watching your children go to school or making their own lives, or accepting that you will not have children. Even breaking out of a relationship that has turned sour can be painful if you look back at the sweet moments.

Death reminds us that life doesn't stand still. We should allow our sadness and memories to emerge and make time to grieve before going on. Regrets and looking back are a vital part of human experience and whatever our loss we owe it to ourselves to talk and if necessary cry a little before going forward.

The negative aspect of Death shows itself when we do

not recognise that it is time to let go. Possessiveness is often rooted in the fear of being alone and sometimes it takes great courage to accept we are no longer the centre of someone else's world.

 Temperance is the card of harmony, balance and compromise. You cannot be responsible for the happiness or success of others nor feel guilty because you can't fulfil their dreams, no matter how much you love them. A lot of people, myself included, lose sleep over what *might* happen and are then too tired to cope when real trouble comes. A year on, the seemingly life-and-death issue we alienated friends and family over turns out not to be as vital as we thought. Of course, we've all got to take a stand sometimes, but Temperance reminds us that for now we need to compromise. Most importantly, Temperance talks about harmony and peace of mind and this can sometimes be best achieved by avoiding confrontation and redressing any imbalance or stress in one area of your life by making positive steps in another.

The negative side of Temperance is a tendency to keep the peace at all costs. Sometimes a short-term truce has a very high price and some people, especially mothers, constantly intervene in family quarrels and end up feeling worse than the combatants. If this is your pattern at work Temperance says: Concentrate on your own harmony and get involved only in vital issues.

The Cards of Light and Darkness

The next three cards help us accept the negative as well as the positive side to our nature. If we can accept the dark as well as the light then we can summon up a lot of energy to make our dreams come true. We can do this not by going back to the beginning again but by starting from where we are and what we are.

The Devil has no power to summon up or draw evil to you. The Devil was a Judeo-Christian concept, a power to be eradicated, in contrast to Oriental and some Western philosophies where evil was the other pole of good and gods of evil, such as Loki in the Norse tradition, were a necessary facet of creation.

Incorporated in many of the demonic images is the goat-footed pagan Pan, the horned god of nature. He represents natural instincts, Freud's id, that if unbridled would destroy the civilised world. Nevertheless, as Freud recognised, the basic instincts are necessary for survival and procreation.

Some cards show a couple chained to each other. Many of us know destructive relationships fuelled by the mutual needs of those involved and sometimes we contribute not only to making but also continuing our own hell. This is the down side of the Devil. It is possible that the few pleasures you get out of a bad situation are enough to keep you there. Or it may be that your confidence is at such a low ebb that you feel you deserve no more. The Devil card is telling you to find someone to talk to after your reading – counsellor, friend, Samaritan or Citizens' Advice Bureau. For now you may even find personal Tarot readings are depleting your energy. If so, don't attempt any psychic or personal psychological activity till you've sorted out the earthly strife.

But in the vast majority of cases the Devil is a very vital card. Every one of us has negative feelings but these need not be a defect. Anger might be one of the seven deadly sins but if it is channelled in the right direction it can be very useful for getting us moving or for dragging us out of a tight spot.

Instead of denying we are angry, we should try to recognise our black moods. They may be a sign that it is time to walk away from a source of strife.

Everyone feels bad-tempered and thoroughly unreasonable at times. If we can release the safety valve before our feelings get totally out of hand, it's much healthier than storing it all up behind a fixed smile or pained silence. If children can see that adults can strongly disagree without violence or, what is almost as bad, silent emotional blackmail, then they too can learn that anger isn't wrong but it must be expressed in a way where no one gets irrevocably hurt either physically or emotionally.

If you get the Devil in a reading, there's probably quite a lot of pent-up anger bubbling beneath the surface and you may be getting headaches or suffering from insomnia instead of attacking the object of your irritation. Let your family know if you have had problems at work or are feeling threatened or resentful – it's not weak to explain why you are silent or niggling.

The Tower, the card of liberation from restriction, looks pretty forbidding. In some packs it is called the Tower of Destruction or *La Maison Dieu* which is not, as literally translated, the House of God, but a corruption of Diefel, the biblical Tower of Babel, built by the descendants of Noah in an attempt to scale the heavens to avenge themselves on God for sending the Flood. As a punishment God sent down a confusion of tongues. In fact, this was in itself a liberation so that diversity, not only of expression, but ideas could germinate to prevent stagnation.

Although the Tower is sometimes interpreted as a portent of disaster, look at it as a prison that is crumbling and it becomes very positive. It's a mistake to think that when your tower collapses you've got to start again from scratch. You are starting with all your experience and achievements. This card is saying that what you see as a setback may in fact be a chance to be free of certain restrictions.

If you get the Tower, then you may have been feeling trapped or just stale. The wind of change may be blowing but a breath of fresh air is just what you need, whether in a relationship, work or leisure. It's a good time to change routines and add new friends and interests to your life.

The down side of the Tower is the urge to quit when the situation is actually far from hopeless. We all know those people who walk away from a setback or sticky patch, find a new partner, job or even family, and five years on find they are making the same mistakes and repeating the old scenarios. The Tower is about rebuilding from where you are.

The Star is the card of making realistic dreams come true, of hope, inspiration and sudden illumination. Stars have been a symbol of promise in many cultures. For the Ancient Egyptians, the appearance of Sirius heralded the annual flooding of the Nile which brought fertility to the parched land. In the same way dreams and hopes are nourished by practical action. For although we are wishing on a star, those dreams most likely to come true are those that we make come true.

You may get the Star at a time when you are starting to

make plans. They may be very long-term and very ambitious – but you are taking real, forceful steps towards a future you want, given the limitations both in yourself and your circumstances.

The negative aspect of the Star resides in not settling for less than perfection and perhaps not making our relationship or job work for us because we feel it is not as exciting or as fulfilling as we imagined. Our dreams have to be anchored in reality and based on all the wisdom and experience we've acquired, maybe even the change in perspective we gained when lightning struck our Tower and we had to pick up the pieces afterwards. So sometimes our dreams have to be realised in a small way and we can only reach the stars inch by inch.

The Cards of Dreaming and Doing

There are only two cards in this section but they represent the union of reason and intuition, of animus and anima, male and female. They are important in coming to terms and integrating the two sides of our nature.

The Moon, at its most positive, talks of our spiritual world, the world of dreams, imagination, visions and our search for something that cannot be pinned down in material terms.

The moon goddess was worshipped from early times in her three aspects that reflected the life cycle of maiden, mother and wise woman: birth, growth, fruition, wisdom, death and rebirth that are mirrored in the seasons. The wolves and dogs seen baying on some of the cards are a primitive call of nature. Crawling out of the water, the crayfish, one of the oldest surviving creatures, who co-habited with the dinosaurs, is the envoy of timelessness. This then is a very special card, containing elements of many of the others.

The Moon suggests that the world of dreams, daydreams and imagination seems more real right now than what is going on around you. Listen to your inner self. There is something that matters to you, some path, whether psychic or spiritual, that calls; you may be afraid your friends, colleagues and family won't understand if you follow it. Give yourself time to dream. We are more than creatures of the everyday world; if you let your inner star guide you for a while then you will return to real life with a new understanding and serenity.

Can the Moon have a bad side? Only if you don't go back to the world. For the Moon, with its soft glow, can also be the card of illusions and kidding yourself that the 'new you' can be created in five minutes. Time and effort form part of the price of any progress.

 The Sun, the card of pure energy, optimism, joy and success in the world's terms, is the alter-ego of the Moon. It speaks of developing your potential, all the untapped or undeveloped talents and unique gifts you have that, at whatever age, can still fulfil many of those dreams seen in the Star.

Developing your potential may involve training or retraining or maybe even completing the training that marriage and the family interrupted. But potential is a very personal thing and isn't tied up with material success. One woman in her sixties I know who had been suffering from hip trouble of years, interpreted the Sun as a signal that she should use a legacy to pay for a private hip operation, a decision she had been putting off for years. I met her a year later striding along the seafront and I didn't need to ask her if she'd made the right decision.

If you get the Sun in a reading, it may be that a new opportunity has presented itself and your first reaction is 'I couldn't possibly'. Why not? Or perhaps you are feeling as if you are waking up after a long sleep and are eager to be on the move. If you are a bit restricted by money or family commitments, see if there aren't still steps you could take towards improving your life in small ways or unearthing some of those hidden talents. Don't wait for the right time — it never comes. Whether you are twenty or eighty, it is never too early nor too late to respond to the call inside you and go for it. The sun doesn't always shine so when you have those golden days, take advantage of them.

So how can the Sun ever have a negative application? Sunlight can be harsh and if it is too intense it can wither lands and burn people. We are only just discovering the cost of sun-worshipping to extremes. It's sometimes tempting to ignore the consequences of achieving a goal at all costs. A desire to succeed, whether for a career, the body beautiful, or simply the perfect relationship, can become an obsession. The Sun can show up all the cobwebs and cracks in your present life, which is good if it is an impetus to improvement but not if it only distresses you.

The Cards of Moving Forward

The final cards in the Major Arcana bring together all the strands of the Tarot journey. The World represents the step into wider horizons which the Fool was going to take at the beginning of the story. Now he/she is taking a step into the known rather than the unknown.

Judgement, the card of reconciliation and spiritual renewal, is often depicted in terms of the Last Judgement. It has very little to do with other people's assessments of us, for most of us tend to judge ourselves far more harshly than others do.

Judgement acknowledges our humanity and fallibility, which can be burdensome. Equally, there are times when we were right but were misjudged. But dwelling on the past can stop us from moving forward. We need to try to put the situation right if it's still retrievable, even if that means acknowledging openly that we did get it wrong. But once that is done, or if it really is too late to do anything, we've got to forgive ourselves, let the past go and move forward. We can't put the clock back, but we will have learned from some of those mistakes, so the experience wasn't in vain.

Equally, we can accept that others may have acted out of ignorance, folly or unhappiness, and hold out the olive branch to them which may or may not be accepted. Judgement is the last bit of luggage so once we have tied up the loose ends and finished the unfinished business we are free.

If you get Judgement in a reading, you may have been feeling regrets over an old quarrel or a missed opportunity. Going over the words you should never have said or failed to say is like playing a worn-out record and the time has come to forgive yourself and others and go forward.

The negative aspect of Judgement is best summed up in the phrase 'against your better judgement', when logic and common sense are warning you not to rush ahead blindly. It's this aspect that stops us relying entirely on intuition, when this meaning appears then you'll know it's time to listen to your head and not your heart.

The World, the card of expanding horizons and limitless possibilities, is a card of movement, whether involving actual travel or being open to new ideas. It is the card of going forward, not necessarily physically or alone, but knowing that you are complete in yourself. Much as you love those around you, there are times when you are happy to be yourself and by yourself. You know now that being alone isn't the same as being lonely and as you come to depend on people less for your emotional fulfilment, real closeness is more possible. Traditional Tarot readers may promise you exotic travel or even moving across water to live or work on the strength of this card. The problem is that if you are promised exotic holidays, or even a house move, you will end up waiting for fate to provide the goods, or worse still accepting a move you don't want because it was foretold.

If you get the World in a reading, then things have started to come together and you can see a way forward. Your horizons are expanding and you have the confidence to stick out for what you want. You know there are no pots of gold at the end of the rainbow; only you and your mind and hands can get things going.

It is difficult to find a negative side to the World. But sometimes we are being swept along by events and may feel that we are losing touch with the people that matter to us. Take time just to be with those you love and get back in tune with what really matters.

That is the end of the Major Arcana. It provides all you need to learn to read the Tarot; learning the rest of the cards adds to the quality of readings. I find the Major Arcana alone useful for looking at the direction of life, and the beliefs, hopes and fears that drive us. These cards are the key to the Tarot.

EXERCISE 5: A Nine-card Reading Using the Full Major Arcana

You may be sufficiently confident to attempt this reading for someone you know slightly less well, but if not read for yourself or a friend or family member. The more readings for different people you can do, the more confident in your own abilities you become.

Shuffle and deal as usual, this time adding a third row. Deal left to right for row 1, right to left for row 2 and left to right for row 3. Turn over the cards in the order you dealt them and look at the whole spread. You may notice certain cards are linked, for example the Star followed by the Sun, or the World after the Chariot. You may want to read the cards in order or prefer, as I do, to look for a key card that seems to hold the core of the answer.

You can use a three-card spread when you are in a hurry or have a specific question to answer, a six-card spread for more detail or a more complex issue and a full nine-card spread for an issue which is not so clear or may involve a major life change.

A SAMPLE READING USING NINE CARDS

Julia, a journalist in her late twenties, has had her house on the market for several months, but is unable to sell. The estate agent has advised her to drop the price by several thousand pounds, but if she does so, Julia will not be able to repay her mortgage. Should she go ahead and hope she can afford higher payments on her next house to make up the shortfall, or abandon the idea of moving? Julia is very eager to move because she has a new job on the other side of the city that makes her daily journey long and frustrating.

Julia picks:

At first glance, Julia's reading might seem very gloomy, but in fact is suggesting an alternative path.

Card 3: Strength. Julia identified the key card as Strength. Julia did not have a time limit to move, although she had seen several houses she liked. She felt that Strength was suggesting that she should not lose her nerve, but hold on for her original price.

Card 1: The Wheel of Fortune. Her new job had been unexpected, but she had hoped to use the increase in salary to offset the higher house prices in her chosen location. Julia recognised that the strains were not all due to travel, but her own uncertainty at much more competitive work in women's magazines.

Card 2: The Chariot. The card of making change and overcoming obstacles by integrating opposing factors promised success. Julia said that her own uncertainty about whether she actually wanted to leave the house in which she was very happy had made her hesitate to try other estate agencies. Often the Tarot will, in answering one question, pose others.

Card 4: The Tower. This card offered further insight — what was the Tower? The house she needed to sell to be free to move? Julia commented that her new job was in a high tower block and she felt very trapped because the other staff were unfriendly and she found the work not as exciting as she had hoped.

Card 5: Death. Julia admitted she was missing her old job on a local paper as she had many friends who lived locally. They had suggested that she should apply for a senior position that would soon be vacant. The reading was moving from the original question – should Julia sell for a lower price, to the deeper issue – did she want to move?

Card 6: The Devil. What negative feelings was Julia suppressing about the house move and her life? She resented that she was being given a hard time at her new job, because one of the established staff was furious when it was given to an outsider, and she was disappointed that her dream job was not working out.

Card 7: Temperance. Harmony and compromise? Julia was reluctant to quit her new job until she felt she had a chance to prove her worth. But she was interested in the senior job at her old firm. Leaving her house on the market at its present price would give her time to settle in her new job or find something else before she had to decide on where to move house.

Card 8: The Star. Offering optimism, hope and following realistic dreams, this did not seem to suggest going backwards, even to a better job at her old paper, because Julia was ambitious and said that she wanted to become a travel editor, perhaps working abroad. Could she perhaps start to write travel features for the magazine, even moving to a different department?

Card 9: The World. This is always a card of going forwards, not backwards, so that Julia probably would move house when the time was right. In the interim Julia needed to expand her horizons, to develop the skills necessary to fulfil her dreams. Perhaps buying a car was an initial step so that the late-night travel would not be such a problem.

Card 3: Strength. In this wider context says that Julia must not lose her courage, but persist quietly but with determination to make a success of her new job and use it as a step towards building her future.

I met Julia some months later. She had sold her house at almost the asking price and had settled at her new job. However, she had just been offered a contract for three months on a radio station abroad and so was waiting before buying a new home in a specific area.

Exercise 6: Beginning Your Personal Tarot Journey

As I mentioned earlier many people identify quite strongly with the Major Arcana cards. Now that you have learned them all it may be helpful to create your own Tarot story.

Begin with the first 11 cards and for each recall a situation where you were, for example, like the Fool stepping into the unknown. If you cannot relate your life easily to the cards, create a figure from any time and place and tell his/her life story using the Tarot sequence. You can illustrate it if you wish. I have given an example below of Jenny who was in one of my classes and felt her life mirrored the Tarot sequence.

Jenny was a young divorced mother, living with her two-year-old daughter Anya. She wrote her story as follows:

The Fool is no problem. I positively jumped off the cliff into the unknown. A sheltered convent school girl, I left college after a year to follow Joe, my musician boyfriend, my first and only love. He was the Magician, older and so exciting, always full of plans and brilliant schemes. Then I fell pregnant and Joe was gone.

The High Priestess I encountered next, for my mother insisted that if I returned home I could not bring the baby. I moved into a small flat and turned into the Empress, totally devoted to my tiny daughter and yet overwhelmed by the responsibility and the sheer hard work.

The Emperor and Hierophant rolled into one were my father who, when I approached him for a loan, left me in no doubt as to the shame I had brought on the family and told me that unless I gave Anya up for adoption he would not help.

The Lovers was unexpected. Will, a kind friend from college days, helped us in so many ways and offered to marry me and be a father to Anya. But I had to steer my own Chariot. I did not love Will and knew in my heart that I would be marrying him for security. Then began a sad time. I felt keenly the injustice (Justice) of my situation and I became the Hermit literally, living only for and through Anya. Then I saw the Tarot classes advertised in the local paper – I do not usually buy it – (The Wheel of Fortune) and felt that although I cannot go out to work, I could manage at least to have a couple of hours away. My mother grudgingly agreed to babysit, so maybe this is a new beginning for us all.

It has taken terrific effort (Strength) just to come

along to the classes when Anya has been ill or my mother has made me feel guilty for leaving my daughter to have fun. I know the Hanged Man because I have given up my youth, but just recently he has taken on new significance. I have seen daytime classes advertised at college and I know there is a crèche.

I have always wanted to go back to university, for the courses here are much more practical and I fancied myself as a scholar. So that has been a sort of Death, accepting I probably won't be a history professor swanning round a tree-lined Oxford college. But Temperance has represented a sort of peace of mind as I have compromised and enrolled for two mornings a week on a Business Studies course.

The Devil has involved letting out the justifiable anger I feel towards Joe for abandoning me. My parents have also done so little and that has actually released my depression. I even told my mother the way I felt. Initially she was angry too and the Tower came down. I did not see her for two weeks but now she has contacted me and seems genuinely to want to get involved with Anya.

The Star has involved accepting that two mornings a week of study are at least a start, and as Anya gets older and can start nursery, I can resume full time education.

The Moon represents the psychic awareness that is emerging as a result of learning the Tarot, giving me the courage to put my life back on track by listening to my inner voice. The Sun is all the ambitions I still cherish: to travel, to become self-sufficient though now I have responsibility for Anya.

Judgement is perhaps the most significant card on

my journey, learning to forgive myself for being impatient and resentful of Anya and above all accepting that I made a mistake out of love and don't need to blame myself for the rest of my life.

The World is not as wide as it once seemed and yet it is wider, because now I and not my parents make my limits. I have college, and I have booked a week's holiday for myself and Anya with the single-parent group we have recently joined. Inch by inch my horizons are widening.

4

Introducing the Tarot Suits & the Minor Arcana

The next two chapters are centred around learning the Tarot suits and the ten number cards in each suit. This chapter deals with the Ace to Four cards and the following one with Five to Ten.

If you have used playing cards, the Ace to Ten in the four Tarot suits should present few problems. As for the four suits, Wands relate to Clubs, Swords to Spades, Pentacles to Diamonds and Cups to Hearts. Once you have learned the Minor Arcana of the Tarot (the Court cards only vary slightly with the Jack of the playing cards split into the Page and Knight in the Tarot), you can then read playing cards just as easily. This is handy if you're far from home as you can buy a pack of playing cards from any newsagent and do an instant reading. Although there are 56 cards, they are not at all difficult to remember once you know both the individual suit and the number meanings.

In the same way that you can read the Major Arcana cards on their own, you can also read the Minor Arcana separately, which is what you will do at first.

The Minor Arcana can home in on specific issues and everyday problems. On some occasions I use the Major Arcana alone for a reading to get the overall picture, then use the Minor Arcana for 'fine tuning'.

Reading the Tarot Suits

Even without learning the individual meanings of the Minor Arcana cards, you could use the Minor Arcana suits as a guide to the major area of concern in your life. Each suit refers to a particular aspect of experience. If one suit predominates in your card readings, then it points to a sphere that may be particularly vital right now although you may not have acknowledged it. We tend not to get nudged by the cards unless an area of our life is overcharged or underpowered.

Pentacles

Pentacles or Discs correspond to the element of Earth and are traditionally linked with money. They are closely linked with the attribute that Jung called sensation, the five senses and above all common sense. They refer to everyday practicalities of life, financial matters and the domestic sphere. A predominance of this suit indicates that progress will be step by step, but results will be real and long-lasting.

You may get mainly Pentacles in a reading when you are working towards a long-term goal and wondering if it's worthwhile carrying on. Pentacles can offer hope; in some ways they are the most positive and satisfying suit of all.

On the negative side, you may be doing too much and feeling overwhelmed with all you have to get through. The solution probably lies in practical remedies rather than in threats or angry words: put forward concrete plans for involving other people and then doggedly enforce the system. Let's look at someone for whom Pentacles provided an early warning of trouble.

Julie is in her early forties and is married with two teenage children. She is also a primary school secretary and finds that she is also expected to bathe wounded knees, change wet pants, wash up the coffee cups and soothe the troubled egos of the staff members. At home she provides room service for her sons and a stress-free environment for her husband. Julie feels frazzled and gets a reading positively groaning with Pentacles.

Never mind the card numbers, we can see the problem and the remedy at once. Julie is doing all the chores for other people who consider what they have to do is far more important than her 'work'. Indeed her husband says she should give up the job and spend more time at home since they don't need the money.

But Julie's job is an important part of her life. So it's time to call a halt and sort out a fairer system at school that involves everyone from the headteacher down having some responsibility for the lower status practical chores that are being assigned to her on the implication that her work isn't as vital as theirs. OK, it won't be easy. Maybe a few days leave might make her colleagues realise just how much she is being lumbered with.

At home, the immediate solution might be a demand to the other family members that either they shell out for paid help (even the teenagers have Saturday job money so can make a token contribution) or lend a hand. A few days of taking to her bed might show the family how much she does.

Cups

Cups or Chalices are linked to the element Water and to our feelings and the relationships so vital to our happiness. They correspond to the attribute Jung called feeling, and symbolise sympathy and a response from the heart not the head. They may indicate a commitment of the heart in the offing or some hidden or unacknowledged turmoil in our relationships with family, close friends and colleagues. Opening your heart to those you love right now is the path to happiness. If in doubt be like water and go with the flow.

If you get mainly Cups then the most effective response to a current joy or sorrow in your life should be what you feel and not what you think. On the negative front, you may be holding back from an emotional issue because of conflicting feelings or fear of being hurt. If in doubt, try to work out what people really mean, which may be the opposite of what they are saying and doing.

For Paul, the large number of Cups in his reading reflected the heartache blocking his path to happiness. He dreaded going home because his partner, Liz, was demanding a commitment in the relationship which he was not prepared to give. They were both in their early thirties and had lived together for five years, enjoying a good social life but keeping their independence, in money and in going on holiday alone when they wanted. Paul couldn't see why she was rocking the boat as he felt their lifestyle was idyllic. But she kept on about wanting to make things permanent.

Paul had ended his previous relationship when his partner had wanted marriage and a family. His own parents' marriage had been a disaster and he had always felt responsible for their unhappiness. He did not want to lose Liz but held back from committing himself in case it spoilt everything.

Even without worrying about the individual cards, we can home in on the situation. Paul needs to listen to Liz; ultimately, he needs to avoid rerunning the old script given him by his parents. Liz naturally believes that his fear of a commitment is a rejection of her and not a response to past pain. He may come to see that emotional commitment is a natural step forward and that the freedom he cherishes is actually holding him back.

Wands

Fire is the element associated with this suit which represents creativity, originality and individuality. This creativity is yours alone, those personal ventures that come from within you and concern your personal happiness. Fire represents the attribute Jung called intuition. Wands is the suit of beginnings, the world of ideas, of energy, excitement and above all action.

A predominance of Wands indicates an exciting time and that you feel full of enthusiasm and maybe a little impatient that others don't share your vision. The solution is to act now and be optimistic.

The negative aspect is an inability to persevere when the initial enthusiasm has worn off and to take on more new projects than you can possibly handle.

Tom was tipped as a high flyer at college. His artwork was exhibited in the annual shows. After college he got a fairly undemanding job in an art materials shop so that he could concentrate on painting. But all he has is a series of unfinished canvasses that friends say are brilliant but which he abandons when the picture isn't as good as he had envisaged. A major exhibition is looming which Tom needs to enter if he is going to make a career of painting. But what is the point, he asks, if his efforts fall so short of the ideal?

Tom, like many Wands people, is his own worst critic. If he really wants to live by painting, he needs to set targets for completing his unfinished works, doing as good a job as he can – not as he dreams of. Then he must submit his creations to public scrutiny in the commercial as opposed to the art-college world to see if he has a future. This will be painful for a perfectionist, but better than a pile of abandoned dreams.

Swords

The element linked to this suit is Air. Jung linked Air with the attribute he called thinking, so Swords are the suit of logic and determination. They speak of limitations and obstacles but also the power to initiate change, especially under difficult circumstances. While Cups tell us to rely on our emotions, a predominance of Swords in a reading say it is time for the head not the heart.

The negative aspect of Swords is a tendency to allow inner fears or past failures to stand in the way of moving forward.

Daniel got mainly Swords when he felt he wasn't steering his own ship of fate. A freelance writer, his tax affairs were in a mess and he had stopped opening those brown envelopes. So how can Daniel avoid the 'curse of Swords'? By opening those letters and visiting the tax office with a set of figures that may show, in fact, he didn't earn very much working for himself. Indeed, he may even be entitled to a rebate. At the worst he can sort out an acceptable way of paying his arrears, rather than waiting for the Sword of Damocles to fall.

Interpreting the Spread at a Glance

What if you get equal numbers of two suits in a reading? Then there may be two different areas of concern that may even be related or demand a two-pronged approach. When one of each suit appears in a reading it may be a time to watch and wait, keeping your options open.

Since Minor Arcana cards outnumber the Major by two to one, in a full-pack reading you'd expect mainly Minor cards.

☆ If you get a higher proportion of Major Arcana cards, traditionally it is said that fate or outside influence has the stronger hand. It can also indicate that the issue under question is a central one and that you may need to take a long-term view.

☆ If the cards are considerably more than about two to one Minor to Major then you have more choice. A predominance of Minor Cards can also point to either to one or a number of smaller specific issues and suggest that it may be helpful to concentrate on a short-term plan.

Interpreting the Numbers

Numerological meanings are also a good indicator (see the *Complete Guide to Divination*, Piatkus, 1998, for an explanation of numerology). These can vary and so you should rely on your own feelings about a card.

The Aces

The number One is ruled by the Sun and is the ultimate beginning and end, source of all energy. Aces are vital and very exciting cards whatever the suit. Beginnings take place thoughout our lives and contain all the energy and enthusiasm of the original Creative One. Indeed, the chance to start again, especially after a traumatic change, can give us hope during the darkest of nights.

An Ace indicates a new beginning or an unexpected change. That is really all you need to remember, then apply what you learned about each suit in the last chapter. In this way it is quite possible to read with the Minor Arcana without learning massive volumes of meanings. However, I will go into detail about the individual cards from which you can develop your own ideas. But do not feel that you must be able to recite my meanings. What is vital is to apply the cards to your life.

The Ace of Pentacles

Since Pentacles are the element of Earth, the Ace involves a new beginning in a practical sphere and promises that success or fulfilment are within our grasp if we are prepared to make that step-by-step effort and not look for instant rewards.

Like all aces, it speaks of change, but on a material or practical level. You may need to change your job or home or learn a new skill, which can be a bit daunting. Give up something you don't enjoy in your life to give yourself time for pleasure; avoid extra burdens in your busy world.

The Ace of Cups

The Ace of Cups represents either a new relationship or a new stage in a relationship, or indeed the beginning of a more spiritual path.

Where feelings and relationships are concerned there are many new beginnings that are as tentative and emotion-filled as any first love. For example, when the last child leaves home, some parents may have put their own needs second for so long that they may have grown apart emotionally and have to get to know each other again if they are not to cling on to adult children or smother grandchildren.

When Cups are involved, it's important to find out what people mean – and it is probably not what they are saying. So you should not start out with any misconceptions or unrealistic expectations that may sour the new relationship, whether a personal or business one.

The Ace of Wands

The Ace of Wands is the first card in the suit of Fire and so the most dynamic. It is about beginning a new venture, putting some dream or idea into action, or formulating an entirely new solution to an old problem. It is the card of pure inspiration and so is a very exciting one to turn over.

To ensure the new plan doesn't run out of energy, remember when you turn over this card that each venture is really a series of new beginnings and that today is the time not only to start but also to keep going.

The Ace of Swords

This is the first card of the suit of Air and heralds a beginning under difficult circumstances, maybe after a business failure or a broken relationship. Except you aren't really at square one in life, because you have learned so much from past failures and hurts. Now you are basing your initial moves on logic rather than hot air. When you've built up your confidence, intuition and inspiration will come flooding back. But for now you are checking and double-checking.

The Twos

These deal with partnerships and balancing calls on our time. The Creative One has split into the Two of Duality and Diversity and is ruled by the moon. In it exist the polarities of light and darkness, good and bad, masculine and feminine, competitiveness and nurturing. Sometimes one predominates or there can be a conflict of interests, but at best we can balance our caring and assertive sides, our negative and positive energies. The twos can warn us when this balancing act is getting out of control.

The Two of Pentacles

 This card talks about juggling work and family commitments with what we want to do ourselves. People do successfully combine career and relationships or work and personal fulfilment, but we can end up feeling frazzled unless we sort out the practical issues.

The Two of Pentacles is likely to appear when you are feeling the pressure of fitting in all your commitments. The answer may be to tackle the most urgent tasks and put the others on hold, no matter how loudly those involved call for your attention. You can only do one thing well at a time so it is important not to fret about the jobs you are not doing or you may feel too exhausted or resentful to do anything.

The Two of Cups

 This card may herald the deepening of a relationship, whether love or friendship, the mending of a quarrel or a period of harmony. On the one hand, it is the card of reconciliation, mending of quarrels, even the coming together of lovers or friends. On the other, it can be the card of conflict, with you torn between two family members or between two sides in a dispute at work.

The Two of Cups indicates that a relationship, whether at work or with someone close, involves a fair amount of emotion so it's important to recognise both the positive and negative aspects so you aren't either over-idealistic or negative, which can lead to disillusion. In matters of the heart it's vital to keep the balance.

The Two of Wands

This is the card of alternatives. Wands indicate a choice between ideas and ideals: whether we want success or personal fulfilment. The card questions if it is possible to have both.

The Two of Wands may appear when your ideals are being tested and there's a choice to be made that involves principles and practicalities. It's about giving up security for satisfaction, an issue the cards bring up again and again.

The Two of Swords

Unlike the last card, this card suggests that you are not that keen on either alternative: piranhas if you go through the water or the tigers waiting in the bush. So you cower in your tent and hope tomorrow may magically offer a solution, which it never does. But you need to look at the facts clearly and coldly, then make an informed decision.

The Two of Swords tells you that doing nothing won't get you out of the sticky situation. So weigh up the pros and cons then go straight for the logical option – even if it is not the easiest route. If in doubt write down the options with the cons and any pros you can find. At least you're doing something to get on the right road again.

The Threes

Threes are thought to have great significance as the number of mind, body and spirit; the number of the Holy Trinity. Therefore, these cards have a strong creative element and represent the achievement of initial goals and hope that whatever has been achieved is a sure foundation for future success. The Threes talk of a short-term result in your efforts. But the result won't last forever, so enjoy or accept what is happening now in the knowledge it will soon be time to move on. The Threes involve co-operation and increase, whether a gain or the need for extra input. They are the cards of unity.

The Three of Pentacles

You may have been putting terrific effort into some practical project and be wondering if it will all be worthwhile. Look around and see your very real if modest achievements. Keep going a step at a time and work with others rather than alone, the key to success at this time.

The Three of Cups

The early Cups cards tend to be associated with birth and marriages and the Three promises celebration, whether a birth or addition to the family, a family gathering, a get-together with absent friends or a period of emotional happiness in the family.

The Three of Cups tells us to accept what emotional happiness or reconciliation we are being offered or even that it's a good time to extend an olive branch in family affairs.

This card may appear when you are enjoying a stable period emotionally or feel that a new relationship is working out well or old strife is about to be resolved. Don't look for guarantees, but be happy for today.

The Three of Wands

This can indicate that a plan has been marked out or a step forward taken, whether towards independence or personal fulfilment. Remember that Wands are the cards of you rather than other people. Your future is very open. Take time to plan your next leap forward.

The Three of Wands marks the widening of horizons, the formulating of definite plans and promises that a period of waiting or stagnation will soon be over. It tells us it is time to look back at how far we have travelled, either spiritually or in making our dreams come true. You may not have done as much as you first hoped but at least you have achieved something. It may be a modest achievement but it is a success you might not have envisaged.

The Three of Swords

The Three of Swords represents the problematic aspect of relationships involving more than two people. The card reminds us that achievement can be painful with unexpected emotional costs. But it is not entirely negative, for sometimes in the process of being hurt we can grow stronger. Even those inflicting those sword wounds on your heart will give up when they see your determination.

The Three of Swords may turn up when you may have been on the receiving end of scorn or emotional blackmail. Keep faith despite the pain; you have survived the worst.

The Fours

The Fours are the cards of organisation and stability. Four represents the earthing or grounding of mind, body and spirit within the material plane. The cards talk about adapting dreams to the world, as it is not the world we should like it to be.

The Four of Pentacles

 This is the card of holding on to what has been partially achieved or attained in a practical or material sense. We may be afraid that if we carry on with a new course of action, we may fail and lose what we already have. 'Be content with what you have' may be a popular maxim, but it can keep us stuck in the same groove.

You may turn up the Four of Pentacles if you are considering a risk: taking a new job, moving in with a new partner, or just leaving the comforts (and restrictions) of home. Your doubts about the enterprise may not be grounded so much in common sense as in the fear that if it all goes wrong you will be worse off. But 'you have to speculate to accumulate' and you must decide whether the danger of stagnating is greater than the risk of losing what you have.

The Four of Cups

 The Four of Cups expresses vague discontent or a general desire for something more exciting, the pursuit of which may put at risk an existing relationship or friendship. It may appear when you are on the point of making or breaking an emotional commitment or feeling swamped by another's emotions. It may be time to share your fears with the other person involved. This is not giving them power over you but a chance for you to work through the future together and accept that all relationships involve some risks and a loss of self.

The Four of Wands

The Four of Wands represents success and recognition of achievement, but prompts the question 'What is the next stage?', for there is an inner restlessness that will not be contented for long. The Four of Wands is telling us not to rest on our laurels. It's not talking about material risks like Four of Pentacles, but about developing your full potential at the cost of ease and comfort.

Having achieved a certain measure of success, whether at work or in a creative venture, it is very easy to call it a day and not worry about your unfulfilled potential. But just ticking over can leave us feeling unfulfilled and restless. This card may tell you there is more to life than comfort and now may be the time to seek your dream and danger.

The Four of Swords

The intimations here are of the ghosts in our head, the fears that may seem very real and which can paralyse us into inaction. The Four of Swords tells us that it is important to sort out the real sticking points and use logic and thought to get round them. Ignore those old miserable characters in your skull and replace them with positive people in the real world who will encourage you. Real limitations can be overcome but not those we allow the spectres of the past to impose.

Exercise 7: A Horseshoe Spread

This five-card layout does assign significance to the position of the cards and this can be of special help in more specific questions or issues. I have listed the meaning of each individual card below. The spread varies according to different practitioners so if the assigned positions do not feel right, experiment until the format works for you. The Horseshoe layout can be used either with the Major Arcana or a complete pack. However the underlying rationale is the same.

You begin at the left foot of the horseshoe with the root issue and then add to this the factors that can help you make a decision, in this case everyone who is involved in creating or continuing the present position. Above that, right in the centre is what you could call the balancing factor, all the unknown influences that when brought to light in the reading can help to create a balanced decision. You then descend down the right foot of the horseshoe to return the matter to the earthly sphere by uncovering a suggested solution through the cards, and finally return to roots in the last card which gives the likely impact of any action on your life.

You may begin with a specific issue in mind or find that if you let your mind go blank the first card dealt will provide the real question. Unlike a three-, six- or nine-card spread, the Horseshoe Spread does not have a key card, but relies on position meanings to build up the picture.

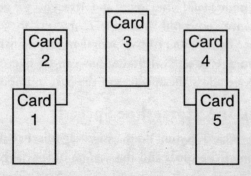

Card 1: *Your present position* and either the choice, dilemma or predominant question about some aspect of your life.

Card 2: *Present influences*. These are all the people and circumstances that have contributed to your present position and who would be affected by any decision or change you make.

Card 3: *Unexpected influences*. These are partly the hidden factors that influence us, past successes and all the messages we carry from parents, past lovers, etc. They also include those factors we can see just beyond the horizon that will come into play according to whether we decide to change or preserve the status quo.

Card 4: *Suggested action* or decision to wait, both of which will alter the path that we would have followed if we had let events or others dictate the future.

Card 5: *Possible outcome* of intervention.

A SAMPLE HORSESHOE SPREAD

Alan is about to retire and his wife Sue wants to go to Australia on an extended holiday to see their daughter and grandchildren, with a view to settling there for at least part of every year. Alan wants to spend a few months relaxing before he does anything and is reluctant to leave the area where they have lived all their lives. Sue says if Alan will not come she will go alone. Alan picks (see over):

Card 1: *Present position and the question* — The Two of Wands. Alan is poised on the brink of major changes: retirement; a trip to the other side of the world; and the

71

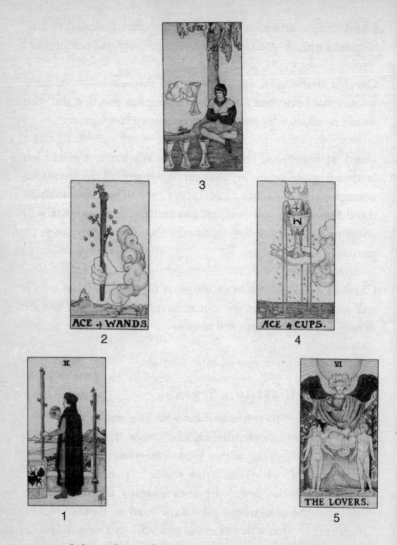

possibility of spending part of every year thousands of miles from home. The card reflects his uncertainty.

Card 2: *Present influences* – The Ace of Wands. Alan's wife and daughter are pressing him to make a new beginning, but he has worked at the same firm since leaving school and feels that the disruption of leaving the job he lives for is enough change.

Card 3: *Unexpected influences* – The Four of Cups. A sudden change from Wands with their emphasis on change and travel to the Cups which deal with emotions and relationships. This card presages discontent and Alan admitted growing apart from his wife since their daughter had left home. He was worried about how he and Sue would cope outside the routine they had established.

Card 4: *Suggested action* – The Ace of Cups. Not a new romance, but a new beginning with his wife, to see if they could rekindle their former affection. Alan decided that he would be happy if they could spend a few weeks at home before the trip.

Card 5: *Possible outcome of action* – The Lovers. This was Alan's first major Arcana card, and suggested that he was taking control of his destiny. The card promised new relationships, with his wife and with his daughter and grand-daughter, once he had resolved his own dilemma of living without work.

Alan and Sue did go to Australia and it was Alan who insisted on returning for a second visit to see his daughter.

EXERCISE 8: Continuing Your Personal Tarot Story

You have already looked at the significance of the first 11 cards of the Major Arcana in connection with your life. Now add the last 11 cards of the Major Arcana. Some people like to weave in the Minor cards as well, but I find that the story works best with the Major Arcana alone.

However, when you learn the Court cards you will almost certainly identify people you know with their characters.

5

Using the Minor Arcana for More Complex Readings

The Fives

These are linked with both communication and versatility. The traditional instability of the Tarot Fives reflects this quicksilver quality. They can encourage us, at best, to question our approach to a situation, communicating our needs and fears; at worst, to give up.

The Five of Pentacles

The card is saying that if we are worried about practical issues, we should communicate our need — but not to a conventional source which in this case cannot or will not help us.

You may get the Five of Pentacles when you are suffering in silence or have found that friends, family and colleagues have been unsympathetic on this particular occasion when you need practical help, not platitudes.

It may be that you're not letting people see what you

really need. Few people are mind readers and many are remarkably slow to recognise vulnerability, especially if you are normally a tower of strength. Perhaps you should look for help from a new source, maybe someone you might not have thought of as particularly friendly or understanding.

The Five of Cups

The Five of Cups reflects a disappointment or emotional setback, but says that it is important to keep this in perspective and see what can be salvaged, as the loss is only partial and may even be restored. All relationships hit down patches and the Five indicates that a lack of communication may be the key.

You may be disappointed in affairs of the heart or a long-standing relationship and be tempted to walk away. Remember the opened wine bottle syndrome: whether you see it as half full or half empty depends on your perspective, but can make all the difference to your response. So look for the positive aspects and, above all, keep communicating.

The Five of Wands

This card may appear when you are wondering if it is worthwhile struggling to fulfil your dream or even carry through an idea or personal plan when it seems to be causing so much opposition. Of course, it's always worth fighting for what you want or believe in and you can even gain extra impetus when you win through.

The Five of Swords

 The Five of Swords implies that the odds may seem insurmountable, but the answer lies in finding another more subtle tactic. Aggression may not be the answer, and that success lies in using the other aspect of the Swords – logic – to defeat the opposition.

You may get the Five of Swords when you have come off worst in a battle of words (reflecting the communication element of the Fives). You feel your cause is just, so you should continue to fight. Muster your facts and figures and go into battle again.

The Sixes

The Sixes are ruled by Venus and reflect peace and harmony and events that turn out better than expected. However, Venus also brings an element of escapism and idealism. So the Sixes reflect not only outer calm, but also an inner peace or need for it because sometimes the Tarot can reflect what we need and desire as well as what is.

The Six of Pentacles

 This is a progression from the miser of the Four of Pentacles; it talks of balance in giving and receiving practical help. Unlike the Five of Pentacles, you may be the one giving and that can be very creative and satisfying so long as you remember also to give to yourself.

If you get the Six of Pentacles in a reading you may find that you are giving out rather more than you are getting back in a practical sense (a quality of the Empress who sometimes cares too much). So it is time to ensure that you are getting help in return from others and, above all, giving time to yourself and your own real needs so that your harmony does not turn to discord.

The Six of Cups

The Six of Cups is the card of nostalgia, of looking back on peaceful, sunlit days, perhaps through rose-tinted spectacles. It may not be too late to rekindle the past. However, this card may also indicate that children or old people can bring happiness to your life.

You may get the Six of Cups when you have been waxing sentimental about earlier times. Perhaps it really was as good as you remember. Or maybe today's relationships are proving less than harmonious and you find yourself wishing you could turn the clock back so that the old romance and magic would return into your world. The only way you'll get them back is by making happiness right now, taking what was good about past relationships and using it to rekindle present joys.

The Six of Wands

This is a card that heralds promotion or recognition of your worth and says that you are on the right path and should not doubt yourself. Your personal path has proved the right one, even if approval is more muted. In the near future your efforts will be rewarded, or at least acknowledged.

The Six of Wands is a clear pointer that you have got the balance right in your life between achieving your own happiness and not hurting others, between work and personal affairs. Go ahead with confidence, knowing that this is the first of many small victories on the way to finding happiness.

The Six of Swords

The Six of Swords says that calmer times are ahead after a period of unrest or uncertainty, so long as you leave behind any bitterness or regrets. This card is sometimes taken to indicate travel. The card may not be talking about a physical journey, it indicates that you need to take steps to move away from any conflict or lingering regrets or doubts.

If you get the Six of Swords it is time to stop worrying over old troubles or fighting a lost cause and, instead, move forward. The important thing is to seek your own peace of mind and that may mean accepting that some injustices cannot be put right and you may not get compensation for wrongs done to you.

The Sevens

The Sevens deal with wisdom acquired through experience, unconscious wisdom and the search for something more than material success. There may be a hint of illusion, for it is a number of dreams and imagination – but dreams can be the first step to finding happiness.

The Seven of Pentacles

The Seven of Pentacles expresses doubts at the sheer immensity of the task undertaken either financially or in the practical sphere. There are no short cuts but it may be important to find temporary respite from money and work worries.

You may get the Seven of Pentacles when you are wondering what it is that you are really working for. The card is not telling you to give it all up and retire to a hermitage to find yourself, but pointing out that perhaps the sheer effort of living has blocked out another important side of you. Pause, rest and reflect. Take a day off or a holiday if you can and your enthusiasm and energy will return.

The Seven of Cups

This card involves the need to choose between several options, between success in the world's terms or emotional satisfaction. It may be necessary to consider the less certain path where emotional and spiritual fulfilment may offer less tangible rewards. Danger comes from choosing none or trying for everything and perhaps losing it all.

If you get the Seven of Cups, it may be that you are at the crossroads. In your heart you know the answer and you should make the decision before life sets you on a path you may not want to take.

The Seven of Wands

The Seven of Wands says you may be finding it hard to stand by your principles or live with people who have very different values, especially if you are facing a lot of back-biting or rivalry. However, your own satisfaction is probably worth more to you than the approval of others. So it is quite a lonely card, but also very positive, for you know that ultimately there's more to life than other people's opinions.

The Seven of Swords

This card warns that there may be less than honest behaviour among those around you. Use stealth to defeat any opposition.

If you get the Seven of Swords in a reading then maybe someone close to you is claiming part of the credit due to you or perhaps even complaining behind your back. This isn't a prophecy – you're no doubt aware of backbiting or unfair gossip. So it is time to tackle the situation using the logic of the Swords after seeing if there is any truth in the accusations.

The Eights

The Eights are the cards of overcoming obstacles and abandoning what may be redundant. They are the cards of positive change, ruled by Saturn and are full of movement, adapting and learning new skills.

The Eight of Pentacles

This is often called the apprentice card and may appear when someone has been made redundant and suggests that the best way forward is developing their skills in a different field.

This card does not just talk about work. It reminds us that in any practical sphere where there has been a setback or change of direction imposed by others, it is important to adapt in a practical way and be prepared to build on our existing abilities in a step-by-step manner that offers a sure foundation for future success.

The Eight of Cups

This is very much a card of Saturn and also the moon in its full to waning aspect, showing that one cycle is moving to an end. If you get the Eight of Cups you may be moving away from a redundant stage in your life. The mountain you must climb may look wild and lonely, but it is a time for courage and looking inward. Strength for others cannot always meet all our emotional needs.

Though the suit is Cups – emotion – it does not have to be a love affair you are leaving. As we saw in the Lovers, family life is full of endings and sometimes only by walking away can we free our children to fulfil their own destinies.

The Eight of Wands

A card associated with travel and moving house, the Eight of Wands talks of a complete change or even turnabout of ideas or beliefs that may involve physical uprooting or a sudden enlightenment or burst of enthusiasm. But you can be fairly certain that some obstacle or setback prompted the new approach.

You may get the Eight of Wands when you have reached a watershed where you need a very creative, inspired approach – perhaps a change of scene or a change of attitudes. It's a very exciting card and promises that if you use your inspiration then no personal or professional setback will hold you back.

The Eight of Swords

This is not a card of blind fate, as is sometimes suggested; it is one of struggling to be free.

If you get the Eight of Swords in a reading you may be feeling very restricted by the demands of others, or by old feelings of guilt that you thought you'd left behind. You've taken the first steps to escape from a stifling situation but it's important not to be trapped on the first leg of your journey by fears within or opposition without. The Swords are the suit of logic so you must use your head, not your heart, to overcome the real obstacles. You can make it if you are strong.

The Nines

These cards talk of action and the courage and determination to succeed whatever the odds. They promote self-reliance, independence or, at their most negative, total isolation. They are the cards of supreme effort. They also speak of independence and perfection.

The Nine of Pentacles

The Nine of Pentacles, known sometimes as the Wish Card, is the card of security and independence, whether in a material sense or a determination not to rely on others to solve crises. It promises material success through one's own resources and efforts.

If you get the Nine of Pentacles in a reading, financial or material independence may be an issue, or perhaps you are anticipating a major practical or financial change, whether a change of job, house or launching a venture that is important to you. Perhaps you have a carefully typed manuscript ready to send to a publisher or you are planning to move home, but are postponing action until after Christmas or when the children are back at school. You need to decide for yourself what it is you really want, even if it is redecorating the house from top to bottom, or you may accept that you are happier as you are.

The Nine of Cups

This is the card of self-confidence and emotional self-reliance, an ability to be happy in one's own company and sure of one's own worth. It can be interpreted as the emotional isolation of one who demands perfection in others and seeks ideal love, not a real person.

If you get the Nine of Cups in a reading, then you may still be searching for the right person or relationships may be temporarily less important than the fulfilment of a particular dream or ambition. Have the courage to follow your heart's desire — as long as you accept that seeking perfection in others can be a solitary path.

The Nine of Wands

This card is often given the title of 'bloody but unbowed'. If you get the Nine of Wands in a reading then you may feel as though you have had to fight long and hard for what you want and wonder if it's worth carrying on. It can be very lonely if you are standing out against the majority. But you've come so far, and success is assured if you keep your courage and determination.

The Nine of Swords

The Nine of Swords reflects, rather than predicts, doubts and despair that have been magnified to the point where no solution seems possible. There may be many problems in the outside world, but only by facing them with courage, breaking out of the isolation and seeking support will you dissipate the darkness.

If you get the Nine of Swords in a reading, then perhaps you too are closing your eyes and seeing past failures instead of the present perils and hesitating from some major decision you know involves conflict. Today's problems are fearsome enough without fighting old foes at the same time, so you must cast them off before moving on.

The Tens

The Tens herald completion, which can either represent perfection, or the need for endings before new beginnings and new hope. These cards of fulfilment are ruled by Pluto who eliminates all that is redundant in our lives. Life rarely stands still and often, as soon as we have arrived, we find ourselves en route to a new destination.

The Ten of Pentacles

 This card shows the culmination of hard work and practical effort and says happiness lies in the domestic world, whether finding the ideal home or making the present one comfortable. The images of the patriarch, family, castle and garden suggest following the conventional path and succeeding and the need to see ourselves as part of a team and not separate.

If you get the Ten of Pentacles then success lies in accepting the traditional and collective approach and realising that what you have achieved is worthwhile. For you at present the hearth and home are far more fulfilling than lonely shores or wild dreams.

The Ten of Cups

 The Ten of Cups gives the same message on the emotional plane. Happiness lies through stable relationships, togetherness and family bliss rather than romantic love and passion. We need to accept relationships as they are, with bad aspects as well as good. This card occasionally turns up when one partner's thoughts are straying.

You may get the Ten of Cups when you intend to make a deep emotional commitment or have accepted that for now the wider family needs your attention. You have a lot to be happy about, so don't pine for what might have been. The card may appear when you are alone but feel it's time to settle down.

The next two cards are much more about 'the end before a new beginning' aspect of the Tens.

The Ten of Wands

 This card talks of a heavy burden or worry that is soon to be lifted. There is a great deal of confusion about what this card says, but the wands seem to represent what has been achieved on the creative, professional or personal front. That is quite considerable as symbolised by the ten wands.

The Ten of Wands may mirror your feelings of frustration and being overburdened. It is a question now of off-loading any unnecessary responsibilities imposed by others and accepting that you have gone as far as you can or should. You should go forward, free of any restricting obligations.

The Ten of Swords

The Ten of Swords is sometimes called the darkest hour before the dawn. But the dawn is breaking and the terrors of the night can be dispersed by the actions of the new day.

You may get the Ten of Swords while desperately fighting a lost cause or hanging on to a dead relationship or stage in your life. It is time to accept that some aspect of your life is ending and allow yourself to be sad and rest before moving on. The sun will shine again for you.

AN OPTIONS SPREAD READING

This is a very useful spread if you have two possible
paths to follow and cannot decide which is best. It uses
the first card you pick to ask a specific question or
identify an area of concern. You then add three cards
below the left and three cards below the right of the top
card to make two alternative paths. The layout should
look like the diagram below. Decide before you deal
which path will apply to each question.

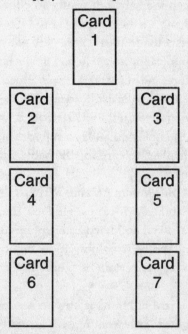

Deal first **Card 1**, the *real issue*.
Card 2 is the *suggested action* for **Option 1**.
Card 3 is the *suggested action* for **Option 2**.
Card 4 is the *unforeseen consequences* for **Option 1**.
Card 5 is the *unforeseen consequences* for **Option 2**.
Card 6 is the *possible outcome* of **Option 1**.

Card 7 is the *possible outcome* of Option 2.
The Options spread works well with the whole pack,
but I have used just the Minor cards to illustrate their
use in a real reading.

A Sample Options Spread Using the Minor Arcana

Richard is in his early fifties and lives with his wife and
sixteen-year-old daughter, Claire, who is pregnant. She
wants to keep the baby but wants no contact with the
father. Richard's wife is prepared to help Claire but
Richard insists that either Claire gets married or puts
the baby up for adoption. He had never had a Tarot
reading before and suspected it was a load of rubbish.

Option 1 was to insist his daughter went along with
his wishes or moved out and Option 2, which he said
was out of the question, was to support his daughter and
wife in their plans to care for the baby. But what was
the real issue?

From the full Minor Arcana, Richard drew first the
Seven of Wands – principles. He feels the standards by
which he has lived and tried to bring up his daughter are
under threat and he is fighting to maintain them. But if
Richard was really certain he would not have agreed to a
reading.

Richard's real dilemma is how to reconcile his love
for his daughter with what he sees as the total betrayal
of his beliefs. The two pathways offer possible solutions
(see opposite).

Card 2 gives a *suggested course of action* for Option 1
(his daughter goes along with his opinions or moves
out). Richard turns up the Eight of Cups – the man

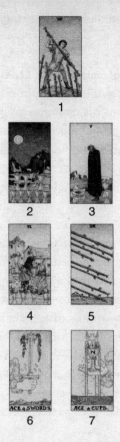

taking the lonely path away from all he has built up. He is contemplating abandoning his daughter but this course may also cost him his wife who could decide to stand by her child rather than her husband.

Card 4, the *unforeseen consequences* for **Option 1**, is the Six of Cups – living in the past and trying to ignore the passing of time. Even if he persuades his daughter to give away her baby, he can't turn back the clock to when she was his sweet little girl. Any attempt to do so

would be an illusion and could bring terrible consequences.

Card 6, the *possible outcome* for **Option 1**, is the Ace of
Swords, a new beginning alone in difficult circumstances. If he forces his daughter to give up her child
and his wife her grandchild for the sake of his
principles then the outcome can bring him only sorrow
and loneliness.

Option 2 is the seemingly unacceptable course of
supporting his daughter as a single parent.

Card 3, *suggested action* for **Option 2**, is the Five of
Cups. Three cups are spilled, but two are still full so
something can be salvaged even though the situation is
far from ideal. The card is saying that if Richard views
events in a positive rather than a negative light, he will
see that there is potential for rebuilding and happiness.
He will gain a grandchild and the satisfaction of knowing
that he stood by his daughter when she needed him and
that his daughter trusted her parents enough to share her
crisis. He could also gain new respect from his wife.

Card 5, *unforeseen circumstances* for **Option 2**, is the
Eight of Wands, the up-and-flying card. Richard may
find that his attitudes become more open as he and his
wife help their daughter. His daughter too may change
her attitude towards the baby's father once she no
longer feels pressured to marry him.

Card 7, the *possible outcome* for **Option 2** is the Ace of
Cups, a new emotional beginning for the family. This
will be a different kind of relationship in which Claire is

seen as an adult responsible for her child and not as a child herself.

Playing the all-powerful parents and shouldering every burden for their child may be holding Richard and his wife back from developing their own relationship. Traditionally this card is associated with a birth, probably because a birth always marks a new stage in a relationship, whether by making parents or grandparents.

Richard did not say much about the reading, except that it was a load of rubbish. Later his wife told me that he had got the old cot down from the loft and was repainting it. For Richard neither option was easy. But if the cards did not offer him a magic solution they at least allowed him to consider a course of action which reconciled his principles with the needs of his family.

EXERCISE 9: Using Earth, Air, Fire and Water Symbols

The Tarot suits can indicate in a reading the nature of an issue, for example an emotional matter might be reflected in a predominance of cups. Each suit carries also an inbuilt strategy:

Pentacles or Discs *(Earth)*. Find a practical solution, approach an issue slowly and cautiously, trusting the evidence of your ears, eyes and common sense, rather than the words of others.

Cups or Chalices *(Water)*. Use your natural empathy with others to see what they mean and feel. If in doubt listen to your heart and your gut feelings. Be prepared to go with the flow and co-operate with others.

Wands or Staves (*Fire*). Rely on intuition and inspiration. Seek a new or unusual approach to an existing problem or challenge and be prepared to explain and sell your ideas.

Swords (*Air*). Believe in yourself and use your head, not your heart. Be prepared for opposition, but if you are logical and ignore critics, not least the old voices in your head.

☆ Before an important meeting or challenge, as well as choosing your card of the day, place the Ace to Ten cards of the four Tarot suits in a single pile and shuffle well.

☆ Cut the cards several times and begin to deal.

☆ Turn the cards until you have an Ace. Lay it out and continue turning until you have other Aces, or cards which can be placed on the Aces (or subsequent cards) in strict card order, i.e. Ace, Two, Three, etc., up to Ten. Your aim is to see which of the four suits is completed first.

☆ If a card cannot be placed in one of the four rows, place it face down on a new pile.

☆ If you have not completed one of the rows before you run out of cards, shuffle the reject pile and continue to deal.

☆ The first row to be completed will give you the correct strategy for action.

6

The Court Cards

There are 16 Court cards, four more than in the playing card deck, because the Jack takes on two aspects, the Page and the Knight. The Court cards can have different names such as Princess and Prince, Daughter and Son and even Priestesses and Shamans instead of the traditional Queens and Kings, but most keep the traditional titles. They usually refer to personalities who are dominant or difficult in our lives, or aspects of our own personalities.

Whether we are male or female, 18 or 80, the aspects inherent in all the cards can be necessary at different times. We all display the power of the Kings at times, when we need to assert ourselves. The nurturing aspect of the Queens can be as vital to men as women. Equally the Knight in us represents enthusiasm for a venture that makes us reckless and more concerned with ideals than actual people or situations. Lastly, the Page can stand for the formulation of a new idea or relationship, or the 'Help, Mum' syndrome where we look to others to bail us out.

The Pages

The Pages are cards of the Earth and may refer to a child or gentle teenager of either sex, or an undeveloped aspect of the questioner's personality. So Pages can be very positive cards. In the Universal Waite pack they are all static figures in the open air, showing that at this stage all things are possible and the direction of the future is undecided. On a more negative note, Pages can represent a person of any age who is childish.

The Page of Pentacles

The Page of Pentacles is a reliable, hard-working and studious young person who is loyal and stoical. What this Page lacks in excitement is made up in reliability. Living always in the real world, he or she is concerned more with doing than thinking. However, this page can be unimaginative and unwilling to try new things.

If you get the Page of Pentacles, you may be glad to be able to rely on someone younger. Or you yourself may be planning a simpler, perhaps a slower way of life. On the other hand, you may find yourself in a practical or financial mess apparently out of the blue and your first reaction is to turn to the friend/bank manager/colleague whom you always lean on in a crisis. Such aid, even if willingly given, does not prevent the same problems creeping up again.

The Page of Cups

The Page of Cups is a dreamer, kind, sympathetic, easily hurt and sensitive to the needs of others, a creature of gentle contemplation rather than romance and passion, and of dreams and daydreams rather than flashes of inspiration. He or she can be unworldly and unable to accept criticism.

The Page of Cups can turn up when you are looking for friendship rather than romance and need to take your time in any relationship. Here your dreams are important in helping you through a mundane or difficult patch, although you must be careful not to spend so much time dreaming that you miss the real thing.

The Page of Wands

The Page of Wands is quick-witted, curious, imaginative and eager to try anything new. His or her ideals are untainted by the desire for success, and enthusiasm for life is unbounded. He stands for the innocent idealism and enthusiasm for life that we all begin with but which, sadly, sometimes gets lost and replaced with cynicism. However, the Page of Wands is easily distracted and becomes discouraged at the first sign of difficulty.

If you get the Page of Wands it may be that a child or younger person is to gladden your heart with their ideals and enthusiasm. The card can also represent a half-formed idea that, as yet, lives only in your head, but may have great implications in the future.

The Page of Swords

The Page of Swords is clever, observant, humorous and aware, even at a young age, of life's limitations and injustices. But his dominating force, fear, which may be unfounded, is holding him back. This uncertainty can make him or her seem devious and careless of others' feelings.

The Page of Swords may appear when someone is masking their insecurity with aggression and needs kindness and reassurance. It is a hard card to deal with because our natural response to an attack is to be hostile in return. But understanding will pay dividends.

You may be hesitating at the beginning of a new venture because of the memory of past hurt and failures. Put the past behind you and one day soon you will be ready for that new beginning.

The Knights

These cards reflect the initial enthusiasm and passion of new relationships and ventures. Knights are often older teenagers, especially boys and men and women in their twenties who may not have formed a stable emotional unit. A Knight can also be a partner or friend of either sex who is adult but still free from responsibility or perhaps not fully mature. But he or she may be a new facet of the questioner which is emerging to take up a cause. The negative aspect is the immature person of any age who pursues his own desires at the expense of others.

The Knights are the cards of Air and are regarded as heralds of news in the area of the next card in a reading. Above all, they are a reminder that the world can be an exciting action-packed place if we just take our courage and cast aside those conventions that restrict us.

The Knight of Pentacles

The Knight of Pentacles is the most stable of the knights, tempering restlessness and crusading with a vein of reality and a respect for the world.

The challenging aspect is that this Knight may lack the vision to explore wider horizons.

The Knight of Pentacles may stand for someone you

know who, although not old in years, does have an awareness of life yet retains enthusiasm and beliefs. If the card is reflecting a facet of you, then you are probably well on course to succeed in whatever venture you are undertaking, as long as you continue to combine common sense with a worthwhile cause.

The Knight of Cups

The Knight of Cups is the original Knight in shining armour. He or she offers excitement, sentiment and romance and his or her quest is for perfection in others – as well as his or her self. His negative aspect is shallowness of feelings and inconstancy in affections.

If you meet the Knight of Cups then your life will not be short of excitement, sentiment and romance. Prepare to be flattered and adored – if you can keep this Knight at your side. If the Knight is a part of you, then you may still be looking for your ideal partner or a fulfilling friendship rather than settling for second best. But do not miss the chance of happiness by constantly scanning the next horizon.

The Knight of Wands

The Knight of Wands is the great communicator and innovator who devises brilliant schemes and loves travel and risk of any kind. This Knight represents perpetual motion. Once he or she gets started there's no stopping him or her. The negative aspect is a tendency to flit from one project to the next, completing nothing. He or she can also be liberal with the truth.

If you encounter the Knight of Wands, you are about to enter life in the fast lane – either under your own steam or propelled by someone close to you. It may also be a time to push through personal projects and to channel your enthusiasm into creative ventures and to fulfilling your potential, so long as you are not diverted.

The Knight of Swords

The Knight of Swords has perhaps the most impetus and determination of all, challenging injustice and showing courage against the most powerful odds. The negative aspect is obsessiveness and a willingness to sacrifice others for his or her cause. The Knight of Swords in your life may be off into battle, leaving you on the sidelines, hoping that he won't get hurt. Perhaps it is time to restrain him – or her – with a little cold logic. The Knight of Swords may turn up when you may feel that you can no longer ignore repeated provocations. But be sure of your facts before you charge, to be certain that you are not letting emotion run away with you.

The Queens

The Queens, cards of Water, represent a more mature woman, whether a mother or a female authority figure, symbolising female fertility and wisdom. They are very positive, creative cards and often appear with the Empress. The Queen is the pivot of many people's worlds. The key to understanding the Queen is discovering what keeps her on that particular throne, necessity or choice?

The negative aspect is in possessiveness or living other people's lives for them.

The Queen of Pentacles

The Queen of Pentacles, sometimes called the Queen of Hearth and Home, is a woman (or man) who deals with practical and financial affairs in such a way as to make all around her comfortable and secure. She is the carer of the sick, the old and the troubled, not by dispensing advice but with practical help.

The negative aspect is that she can become obsessed with order or take over the responsibilities of others and become a martyr.

The Queen of Pentacles points to someone close to you who provides security and comfort. Of you may be caring in practical ways for family, friends or colleagues whether at work or home, and are central to the well-being of others.

The card warns us that you may end up providing the practical or financial back-up for all those Pages who call for help every time a problem looms. Do we encourage other people to rely on us because otherwise we would feel redundant?

The Queen of Cups

The Queen of Cups is naturally intuitive and peace-loving, totally in tune with the feelings of others and the natural world. She represents fertility and creativity in their widest sense. Her challenging aspect is in emotional possessiveness and in seeking ideal rather than real relationships. Here is the universal agony aunt, the ever-smiling peacemaker between friends, relatives and work colleagues.

It is hard to find drawbacks in the Queen of Cups although, in a real crisis, it's easy to take over too many of other people's responsibilities, letting them off the hook, and occasionally getting emotional satisfaction through other people's relationships, rather than your own.

The Queen of Wands

The Queen of Wands is the wise woman, independent, authoritative but also intuitive and imaginative. She is at the hub of activities with her enthusiasm and ability to weld together disparate people and interests, but she does not live through her family, though she may be happily married and a mother.

She is sometimes wrongly labelled the Queen of Hearth and Home – her black cat is a symbol of magic not domesticity, and she has the sunflower and the lion to remind of her links with Fire. Her negative aspect is in her impatience with those who seem weak or lack vision and her inability to let others take the lead.

The card appears when you, or someone close to you, is at the centre of organising schemes that affect those around you. And you know that, although life can get frantic with all the conflicting demands on your time, you are achieving positive results.

The Queen of Swords

The Queen of Swords is the disappointed woman, whether in relationships or the workplace, whose own past or present sorrows can make her bitter and over-critical. Love and kindness still exist beneath the surface, however, and she may prove an unexpected and powerful ally in adversity. Her challenging aspect is her inability to express love and gratitude, and in being unforgiving. She is sometimes associated with divorce, widowhood and even illness, but whether she is someone close or part of you, her key is responsibility and caring in times of difficulty for she is the Queen of sad times either her own or of those she loves.

You may get the Queen of Swords when you want to protect someone who is unhappy or in difficulty, but you know that going into battle on their behalf won't help and you must wait till they ask. Don't underestimate the support your presence gives.

Even the negative side of the Queen of Swords is not malicious. Perhaps out of desperation or sheer unhappiness, the Queen is tempted to resort to emotional blackmail when she should be letting go of a no-win relationship.

The Kings

The Kings represent mature or older men or male authority figures. They embody power, achievement, paternalism and responsibility. If you do not recognise the King in your reading as someone else, it may represent your own animus – your desire and drive to succeed. These qualities can give you a boost if you are wondering whether or not to go ahead with something. The cards of the Fire element talk of power and responsibility; like the Queens they can refer to male or female, young or old. Some people automatically associated a King with their father or boss or husband just as they see the Queen as a mother figure.

The Kings' challenging aspects are domineering ways and inflexibility.

The King of Pentacles

 The King of Pentacles has succeeded either financially, in business, or in a practical, methodical way. In addition, he is firmly rooted in his domestic world of which he sees himself as benign Lord and Master. He works hard for family or to make a comfortable base; he is honest and generous. He is the friendly bank manager, the honest estate agent or wise older person who tempers experience with compassion. His negative aspects are that he can be over-cautious, obsessed by detail and materialistic or so involved in work that he forgets those for whom he is working.

This card indicates concern with security and achievement in worldly terms. There is nothing wrong with wanting the best for ourselves, those we care for, or in working determinedly at a goal. The card says it is important to be single-minded, watch financial matters closely and pay attention to detail to ensure long-term prosperity.

The King of Cups

 The King of Cups is the most approachable of the Kings. Popular and benign, he puts people above property or achievement. He may be spiritual or involved in the caring professions, but is invariably the dreamer who believes in the goodness of humanity to the end of his days. At his best, this is a card where family and partners can feel secure because the King is happiest supporting and pretecting those he loves.

His negative aspects are sudden bursts of anger and flirtatiousness because of his lifelong struggle for ideal love.

This King may appear when you are contemplating a serious commitment. If there's a choice between permanent love or excitement, between the King or Knight of Cups, opt for mature love. Or you may know this King and worry about money and his non-competitive attitude; value his caring qualities, but make sure he does not spend so long helping others he forgets those closest to his heart.

The King of Wands

The King of Wands is a man of vision and ideals, persuasive, an expert communicator and driving force behind many ventures; energetic, optimistic and eager to share his considerable knowledge and wisdom. He lives life to the full and expects others to do the same, loves travel and may move house frequently. This the card of career and ambition! His negative aspects are selfishness and lack of long-term commitment.

If you get the King of Wands in a reading, then achievement in a chosen field is your driving force or that of your particular King of Wands. It's a time to be assertive and overcome opposition or inertia in others with energy and enthusiasm.

The King of Swords

The King of Swords may appear totally rigid and lacking sympathy with humanity, but his strong sense of responsibility and clear thought enable him to succeed. This King is associated with authority figures such as government officials, judges, lawyers and doctors, both men and women.

His negative aspects are pedantry and calculated cruelty to opponents.

If you get the King of Swords in a reading then it is a time to be determined and cool-headed. Make judgements based on logic, not emotion. If you are living with a King of Swords whose constant criticism is destroying your confidence, you should fight back with logic and refuse to be browbeaten. Most Kings of Swords will back down if challenged.

A Court-Card Reading with the Jungian Spread

This method of reading is inspired by Jung's theory of the archetypes, the ideal figures that we carry within us such as the wise father and the good mother which we can find represented in the Major Arcana. It is especially useful for looking at relationships or sorting out why you keep finding yourself in the same position. If you can look at the unconscious influences on you, the voices of these ideal characters in your head, it is often easier to see the best way forward.

You can try your Jungian spread with the 16 Court cards alone, the Major Arcana alone, or perhaps best of all, the 16 Court cards and the Major Arcana. It does not work well with Minor Arcana cards alone. Deal as usual, placing **Card 1** in the centre of the table.

Now make a square surrounding the first card, dealing clockwise so that **Card 2** is directly above **Card**

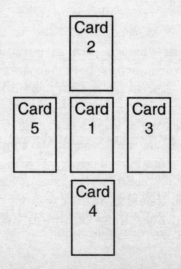

1, **Card 3** is to the right of it, **Card 4** below and **Card 5** to the left of **Card 1**.

Place the cards face down, and turn over each one and read it before revealing the next card.

Card 1 is your *key or predominant pattern* card. This represents the predominant issue that is influencing you, not for all times but perhaps over the last few days or weeks. You may even have noticed it in your dreams.

Card 2 is your *animus card*, the way your competitve, assertive, masculine, logical side is affecting your life and decisions right now. Or it may represent the forceful argument of others. Don't be surprise if a Queen or Page turns up here — you may be finding it hard to get tough.

Card 3 is your *anima card*, the nurturing receptive side of your nature, or mothering people that may either be helpful or smothering. A Knight or King suggests a conflict of interests forcing you to hide this gentler side, perhaps if work is particularly hostile, or everyone is depending on you.

Card 4 is the card of your *shadow side*, the hidden fears or hostilities in your life. This is an important aspect of our personality; negative feeling channelled in the right way can be a strong impetus for change.

Card 5 completes the circle. This is the *inner child*, the real essential you, what you really want and feel whether on a physical or spiritual level, free from the expectations and demands of others.

Sounds complicated? Follow the 16-Court-card reading below and it will become clearer.

Lucy, a wife, mother and grandmother (I stress the three aspects because she has heavy duties in all three roles) is dreading Christmas because she spends the holiday refereeing family disputes as well as providing the food and festivities. This year she has suggested to her husband they go away to a hotel and let the family get on with it, but no one will hear of changing tradition. This was her reading:

Card 1, the *key card* or *predominant pattern*, is the Queen of Cups which represents Lucy feeling responsible for her family's Christmas happiness. The task she took on when the children were young has become a role she increasingly dreads.

Card 2 represents the *animus*, the logical, assertive side of Lucy. What common sense tells her to do is not easy when her emotions lead her in another direction. The Knight of Wands makes a surprise appearance, telling Lucy she should abdicate responsibility and go for personal fulfilment.

Card 3, the *anima*, the caring, nurturing side, is the Queen of Pentacles, giving unconditionally to the extended family of children and grandchildren. But should Lucy be the only one to fill this role when her grown-up children and her husband could help? Perhaps they feel Lucy does not want their help.

Card 4, the *shadow side*, is the part we keep hidden because we think other people won't like the true person

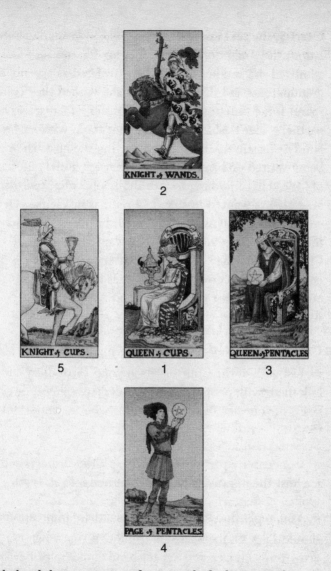

behind the constant smile. Lucy deals the Page of
Pentacles. This can be read two ways, but the underlying
message is the same. Either Lucy resents waiting on everyone else or she would like to be nurtured at Christmas.

Card 5, the real Lucy, the *inner child*, was another reve-
lation, the Knight of Cups. A longing for romance? Lucy
admitted she and her husband only related as parents or
grandparents and that deep down she wished they could
spend some time together re-establishing themselves as
partners. Her husband was reluctant to do without his
family Christmas – he enjoyed playing the host while
being waited on hand and foot. After his initial objection
of 'We'd have nothing to talk about', he admitted that
he'd always wanted to spend Christmas in Vienna. Of
course, the family weren't pleased, but the change gave
them a chance to think how they wanted to spend
Christmas and they actually said afterwards that they had
enjoyed it; deep down the festivities had become an
outworn habit that no one knew how to break.

EXERCISE 10: Fitting the Court Cards into Your World

☆ List each of the Court cards in your Tarot diary and
link them with people in your immediate sphere, or as
facets of your personality, or people who are important
to you.

☆ Concentrate particularly on the positive aspects and
see how the negative side can be turned into strength.

☆ You might find it useful to record these impressions
and see how they change over the months.

☆ You may find that you occupy more than one card
role, according to the relationship and situation.

☆ Note too who you would like to be – many a Queen

of Pentacles is an embryo Queen or even King of Wands.

☆ When you meet someone new, see which Court card they most closely resemble and the card in which their reactions cast you.

☆ Subtly change your own card and see how that brings about a change in others.

7

Readings Using
the Full Pack

Most readers have two or three favourite spreads. However, the more complex Celtic Cross is one regarded as a sign of an expert Tarot reader; it is worth trying, for a very complex issue or an in-depth life review. It is not complicated to learn if you divide it into its three natural sections, then put them all together. It works equally well with playing cards (see the *Complete Guide to Divination* in the Further Reading section) and is sometimes called the Gypsy Spread as it is very popular among Romany clairvoyants.

The Celtic Cross

The *Celtic Cross* is best read with the full pack. Shuffle and deal the cards into three piles and pick from one or deal straight from the pack. Place the cards face down and turn them over section by section, and read each section before looking at the next. When you have read all the cards, put them together to determine a possible solution to the issue.

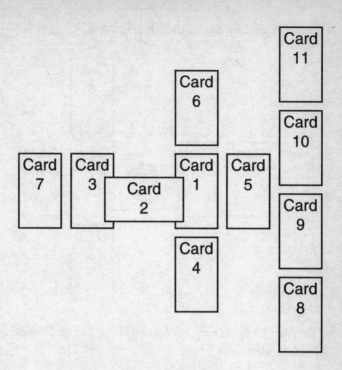

Section 1: The Centre of the Reading

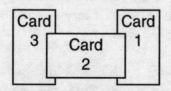

Card 1 represents the *present position*, the circumstances surrounding the issue or question, including past matters that have led to the current situation.

Card 2 represents the *issue dominating your life* or *the question you wish to ask*.

Card 3 represents *obstacles to happiness or success*.

Section 2: The Surrounding Square

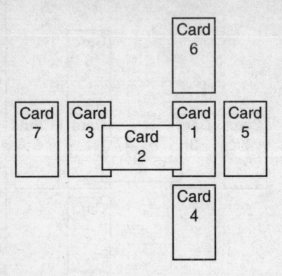

This area represents the underlying factors, based on the ancient elements.

Card 4, *Earth*, is the root of the matter, dealing with the practical considerations that may offer the key to a current problem or planned change.

Card 5, *Air*, is the logical factor that can separate what is possible from what is unrealistic and help to identify your strengths and potential.

Card 6 is the inspirational or *Fire* factor, the 'off the top of your head' insight that can make the missing connections in the equation. It can also reveal hidden dreams and needs.

Card 7 is *Water*, the heart of the matter card, revealing what is going on under the surface, both in your own life and the worlds of those involved. It can also reveal your true feelings, which may be very different from what you consciously thought you felt.

Section 3: Pathway Cards

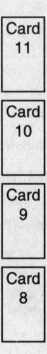

Card 8, *suggested action*, involves a possible change or choice you may make.

Card 9, *helpful influences*, represents people or circumstances that can make the action or decision more likely to succeed. These influences may be unexpected.

Card 10, refers to the *short-term outcome* of any change or action in Card 8.

Card 11, the *long-term outcome*, may be very different from the short-term effects and needs to be considered in deciding if perhaps short-term sacrifice or possible disruption is worthwhile.

A Sample Celtic Cross Reading

Susan is in her fifties and has an elderly mother who has recently been widowed. Her mother is eager to move in with Susan but, since they have never been close, Susan doubts the arrangement will work, especially as her mother will be moving more than a hundred miles away from her home and friends into the depths of the country. She draws the following sets of cards:

The Centre of the Reading

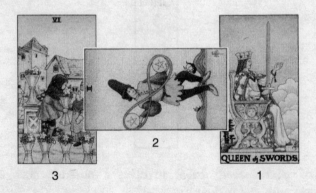

Card 1, the *present position*, the circumstances surrounding the issue or question: The Queen of Swords.

Card 2, the *issue dominating your life* or the *question you wish to ask*: The Two of Pentacles.

Card 3, *obstacles to happiness or success*: The Six of Cups.

Susan's mother, the Queen of Swords, is naturally deeply unhappy. But even before she was widowed, Susan's mother was a disappointed, bitter woman who resented the fact that Susan, her only child, had not followed a conventional path of marriage and children, but had become a photographer living in a remote area of Wales.

The Two of Pentacles concerns the immediate problems of how Susan could accommodate her mother into her busy life when she might have to go off for weeks at an end to a remote area of the world. But Susan felt it was her duty to take on her mother.

The Six of Cups, nostalgia for the past, is a significant card. Both Susan and her mother hope, in their own way, to turn the clock back; Susan's mother to the time when Susan was a compliant child, the centre of her universe, Susan to the early relationship with her mother that she hopes might be rekindled.

The Surrounding Square

This looks at the Underlying Factors (see next page).

Card 4, *Earth*, is the root of the matter, dealing with the practical considerations: The Lovers.

Card 5, *Air*, is the logical factor that can separate what is possible from what is unrealistic and help to identify your strengths and potential: Judgement.

Card 6 is the inspirational or *Fire* factor, the 'off the top of your head' insight that can make the missing connections in the equation. It can also reveal hidden dreams and needs: The Eight of Wands.

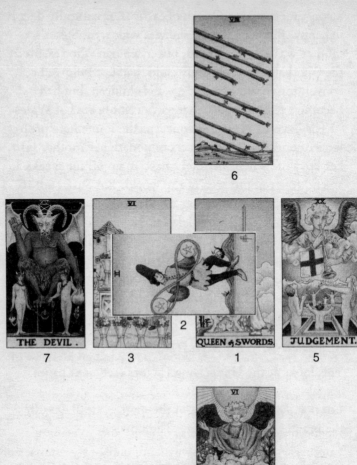

Card 7 is *Water*, the heart of the matter card: the Devil.

The Lovers in the Earth position occupies its role as the

card of relationships. It suggests that Susan and her mother have got very stereotyped ideas of each other and perhaps need to look at the practical as well as emotional implications of living together after so many years apart.

Judgement in the Air position talks of Susan's assessment of herself, her unwarranted guilt at not being what her mother wanted – the dutiful daughter – and her mother's judgement that Susan should now take care of a mother who is still hale and hearty and has a very distinctive life-style based around her bridge parties and golf, neither of which she will be able to pursue in Susan's home.

The Eight of Wands in the Fire position would not seem to refer to the projected move by Susan's mother since this had already been suggested, but an inspired solution. Susan was puzzled, but then said that she had suggested her mother accompanied her on a six-week trip to the US where Susan would be taking pictures of Navajo Indians in Arizona. Her mother had initially dismissed this but Susan felt she could be persuaded and said that it would give mother and daughter a chance to spend time in each other's company and give Susan's mother a chance to get away from unhappy memories of her husband's recent death.

The Devil in the Water position talked of suppressed emotions: Susan admitted that she felt very resentful of her mother's coldness over the past years, despite her efforts to keep in touch, and felt it unfair that her mother just assumed she would change her life to accommodate her.

Pathway Cards

Card 8: *Suggested action*. This involves a possible change or choice you may make: The World.

Card 9: *Helpful influences*. Unexpectedly helpful people or opportunities: The Six of Swords.

Card 10: *Short-term outcome*. This refers to the outcome of any change or action in Card 8: The Six of Pentacles.

Card 11: *Long-term outcome*. This may be very different from the short-term effects and needs to be considered in deciding if perhaps short-term sacrifice or possible disruption is worthwhile: Temperance.

The World in the position of suggested action is another travel card, so that Susan's idea of taking her mother on a working trip, perhaps extended into a holiday, would give both of them breathing space to talk over their future in new surroundings. Susan said she had not had a holiday for two years and had been thinking of taking one.

The Six of Swords in the position of helpful influences or opportunities strengthens the idea of travel, using the image of moving into calmer waters. Susan has not had chance to grieve for her father so the time away will offer her mother the opportunity to help her daughter. Susan's own feelings had been a factor not even considered.

The Six of Pentacles in the short-term outcome position tells Susan what she already knows; that in the short-term she will need to give a great deal of practical support to her mother. But this may avert a long-term crisis if Susan's mother comes round to the idea of seeing her daughter for pleasurable holidays rather than to live with.

Temperance is the long-term outcome, promising that Susan and her mother will find harmony and peace of mind. The cards do not say whether Susan's mother will remain in her own home, because that will depend on Susan living through the experiences touched upon in the reading and then coming to the conclusion that will make them both happy.

EXERCISE 11: Tarot Cards and Meditation

Each of the 78 cards reflects a different facet of ourselves and our lives. One of the most powerful ways of understanding the wisdom that lies behind the cards is to select a single card from a face-down shuffled pack and use it for meditation.

☆ Meditation is best carried out in the evening, when there is time and quiet, but for those who prefer it meditation is also effective in the early morning.

☆ Eat a simple meal as light-headedness can induce dizziness and actually blur focused inspiration. Have a leisurely bath using between eight to ten drops of essential oils that encourage psychic awareness. Either mix three drops of combined oils, such as bergamot, geranium, neroli and ylang-ylang, or use eight to ten drops of a single oil, for example lavender or rose. Place the oil in the water after the bath has been filled so that the oils float on the surface. After your bath slip on something warm, but loose and light.

☆ Light a circle of candles in soft pink or lilac, colours of the spirit, so that you can see your card without artificial light.

☆ Sitting comfortably, tense by placing your hands behind your head; clasping your hands, pull your elbows forward close to your face, so that your hands are taut and you are exerting gentle pressure at the base of your skull. Release your hands and stretch slowly upwards and backwards, like a cat or child awakening from sleep.

☆ Breathe in slowly, hold for three and exhale through the mouth with a sigh. Do this five or six times. Visualise as you inhale the air as pure white or golden light, radiating through your body. Visualise yourself exhaling black mist, leaving your body lighter and more harmonious.

☆ Slow your breathing a little further – one and two and three – seeing that lovely golden or white light entering. Hold your breath for three seconds – one and two and three. Breathe out slowly – one and two and three – so that the dark breath leaves. Then wait for three seconds – one and two and three – and breathe in, repeating the pattern about half a dozen times at first, until the exhaled breath is in your mind's eye, paler and paler and all the negativity has gone.

☆ Hold your chosen card an outstretched arm's length from your face in your cupped hand and let the light and your golden breath surround the card so that the image becomes larger until you are within it.

☆ When you feel you have absorbed every detail, put down the card, close your eyes and walk along the pathway or move behind the throne through a door.

☆ Let yourself progress beyond the card into the world

of those who inhabit it, until you become aware it is time to return.

☆ Go back along the path you took, remembering to thank the character who owns the card for allowing you to enter his or her world.

☆ When you open your eyes, write or sketch in your Tarot book the path of your journey.

☆ You may find you return to the same card again, where you will discover new avenues.

☆ Let your unconscious mind guide you to the *right* card each time you meditate by selecting a card unseen from the pack.

☆ You will find that it answers a specific question.

☆ If you meditate once a week, you will find that your Tarot journeys are enriched by earlier experiences; you may hear your characters speak or smell the perfume of the flowers or hear the birds.

8

Using the Tarot to Explore the Future

The Tarot can be used for planning ahead by marking regular points in times, weeks for short-term changes and months for a longer view. Using our intuitive powers, we can tune into these relevant change points along our future path. The time spreads are not predicting a fixed future, for that is ours to change by our actions and reactions at every stage. Rather it is indicating that certain trends will be present. The very act of discovering these change points allows us to anticipate our destiny.

A Six-Weeks-Ahead Nine-Card Spread

If you have a particularly momentous few weeks ahead or need to make a number of decisions, use the Tarot to tune into these key points.

☆ Six is a good number but you can try fewer or more weeks as long as you remember to include the first and last two cards of the spread.

☆ Use the full pack, or if you prefer, the Major Arcana cards, the Court cards, Pages, Knights, Queens and Kings and the four Aces, 42 cards in all.

☆ Deal nine cards face down, as shown in the diagram below, and turn them one at a time, reading the first then turning them in order.

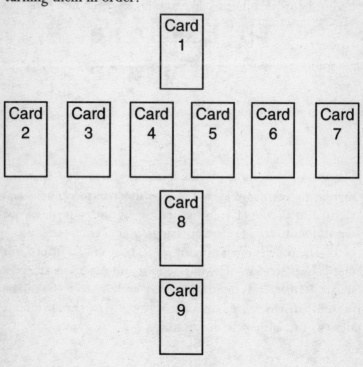

Card 1: *Where I am.*
Card 2: *Week 1.*
Card 3: *Week 2.*
Card 4: *Week 3.*
Card 5: *Week 4.*
Card 6: *Week 5.*
Card 7: *Week 6.*

Card 8: *Where I would like to be.*
Card 9: *The key to the long-term future.*

A Sample Six-Week-Ahead reading

Barry was about to leave college after completing a
social sciences degree, but did not have a job. He did
not know whether to take a temporary job at a local
pizza parlour while he job-hunted, to take a higher
degree, or to try something completely different while
waiting for a post in social work to come up. He drew:

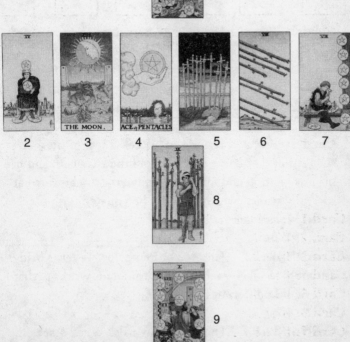

Card 1: *Where I am* – The Seven of Cups.
Card 2: *Week 1* – The Four of Pentacles.
Card 3: *Week 2* – The Moon.
Card 4: *Week 3* – The Ace of Pentacles.
Card 5: *Week 4* – The Ten of Swords.
Card 6: *Week 5* – The Eight of Wands.
Card 7: *Week 6* – The Eight of Pentacles.
Card 8: *Short-term future* – The Nine of Wands.
Card 9: *Long-term future* – The Ten of Pentacles.

Card 1: *The card of where Barry is* – The Seven of Cups.
Barry is uncertain of what he really wants with his future
– the Cups refer to his commitment to the caring
professions. The danger is that unless Barry makes definite plans, he may end up with nothing.

Card 2: *Week 1* – The Four of Pentacles. Another card
of uncertainty for Barry's first week. Should he go for
the safe option, returning to university for another two
years or should he, as was his ambition, begin to work in
the field, but risk not getting a job immediately?

Card 3: *Week 2* – The Moon. Week 2 brings the
suggestion that Barry should avoid the easy path and use
his imagination and innovative powers to achieve what
he really wants, which may not be equated with success
in the world's terms.

Card 4: *Week 3* – The Ace of Pentacles. Week 3 brings
attempts to take practical steps to obtain work, perhaps
in a slightly different field.

Card 5: *Week 4* – The Ten of Swords. Week 4 sees the

setting in of disillusionment if the going gets hard, but says that the darkest hour is before the dawn and if one door closes, there are others to try.

Card 6: *Week 5* – The Eight of Wands. An unexpected change of venue, travel and new fields which if embraced, will bring happiness.

Card 7: *Week 6* – The Eight of Pentacles. Week 6 has the apprentice card, suggesting Barry may be learning a new skill related to his world, but involving hard work, adapting and being pentacles, promising slow but sure success.

Card 8: *The short-term future* – The Nine of Wands. The 'bloody but unbowed' card promises that if Barry accepts that the first few months will be difficult he will succeed.

Card 9: *The key to the long-term future* – The Ten of Pentacles. The card of the long-term future confirms that, if Barry perseveres, he will find financial security and satisfaction in his work, helping others in a practical way.

About two months after the reading, I met Barry who was home for the weekend. He was exhausted but happy. After his initial indecision, he had decided to go for the safe option, returning to study. Then he saw a job advertised working for a charity sending aid to India. This fired his imagination. He applied, but was only offered part-time work which was all the charity could afford. Barry then became very depressed, giving up his charity work to take a full-time job in the pizza parlour.

But before he made these changes, he was invited to go out to India for a few weeks to help the charity to deliver aid and build a clean-water scheme. This involved a crash course in plumbing and irrigation, which he had to fit in with his part-time job. When I met him he was about to set off for India. If things went well, he might be offered a full-time post at the head-quarters of the charity in London, 200 miles away.

A Calendar Spread

Slightly more complex is a Calendar Spread with a circle of 12 cards, plotting the salient features for the year ahead. Use the full pack of 78 cards.

☆ Shuffle. With cards face down, begin your calendar circle with a card for the present month in the 12 o'clock position. Lay down in turn 11 more cards for the year ahead.

☆ Turn the cards over one at a time and you may see a month-by-month pattern emerging.

☆ Record the calendar spread in your Tarot diary and make notes each month and see how far it links with the months ahead.

A 25-Card Spread for Past, Present and Future

This is the most comprehensive spread in the book and one that is best for a major life review at a point when change seems inevitable. Initially I was very doubtful about the effectiveness of such a large spread, but some years ago a friend called Pat did a reading for me using 30 cards and it has been startlingly accurate in every detail.

The 25-card reading spans the dimension of past, present and future and more than any other layout clearly reveals the close connection between them.

Although it involves so many cards, it is very easy to deal, being simply eight cards for each dimension and a final card which crowns the reading and holds the key to future happiness. It is not a spread to hurry, but to read either alone or with a good friend as dusk falls, sitting by candle-light in that half-dream state where the dimensions naturally move close together.

☆ Use the full pack. Only use this spread once for yourself and once for other people, taking time to sit with the cards and describe each one on detail. Shuffle and deal the cards face down as usual, with three rows of eight, from left to right, three times.

☆ The row nearest to you or the person who is dealing their cards is the past, the second the present and the third the future.

☆ Turn over the cards a row at a time, beginning with the past. Read the first row before turning over the second and finally the third. Read each row from left to right letting the cards unfold like steps.

☆ When you have read the row of the future, deal a final card face down from the pack and turn it over. This card represents the *key to happiness*. Once you have read it the rest will fall into place. The *key to happiness* card can be added to any spread if the reading seems incomplete, once all the existing cards in the spread have been read.

EXERCISE 12: Using a Pendulum to Select Tarot Cards

A pendulum, whether a conventional crystal quartz on a chain, a key on a piece of cord, a plumb bob or a favourite pendant, is a tangible expression of your intuition. It can be used to answer questions and is a very effective way of tuning into your deep wisdom. In a Tarot reading, a pendulum will confirm the rightness of your interpretation. When you are feeling uncertain as to the significance of certain cards, your pendulum will vibrate gently over the key cards and you will hear as an inner voice unravelling the significance. The pendulum operates entirely through your psyche, and your unconscious hand movements that control it are a sure guide as your personal wisdom merges with the collective knowledge of mankind. You can use a pendulum with Tarot cards in several ways and it is especially effective if you are reading for someone else and he or she cannot identify with the cards.

Collect the cards into a pile and place them in a circle. This will work whether you are doing a reading of six or nine cards or a set spread with assigned positions. You are not doing anything wrong. It may be that the spread cannot express the particular issues or strategy.

Shuffle the cards from the reading and lay them face down. Give the pendulum to the person for whom you are doing a reading and ask him or her to pass the pendulum slowly anti-clockwise around the circle, beginning in the 12 o'clock position, pausing over each card to unblock the energies.

The pendulum should then be passed clockwise slowly over each card, asking the person to indicate over which card the pendulum is pulling downwards most strongly. The pendulum can be passed around the circle two or three times if the choice is not immediately felt.

Take this first card and place it in a row on the left nearest the questioner. Next ask the person to select a second and then a third card from the circle and place them next to the first card. Ask the questioner to turn over the three cards and these provide the key to the reading.

Usually it is not necessary to select any more cards but if the questioner wishes to do so, use the pendulum method until the required number of cards are selected.

9

Perfecting
the Art of
Tarot Reading

You now have acquired all the knowledge necessary to read
the Tarot. The Further Reading section suggests books you
can read to acquire more background and to learn alternative approaches. The most important skill is to master the
meanings and at least one or two spreads so that they
become automatic.

☆ Write down again and again what the individual cards
mean and lay out cards in sample spreads. Like any skill,
once you have mastered the basics, you can apply your abilities to the real world.

☆ If books give conflicting advice – which inevitably they will
because Tarot reading is such a personal art – establish in your
own mind the core meanings. Try these in reading after
reading and you will find that you have internalised each card
in a unique way. Record your meanings in your Tarot journal.
As you use the Tarot you will modify these meanings and this

is a process that will and should continue all your life.

☆ Above all, leave this and other Tarot books at home when you are giving readings, even in the early stages. It is better to use an unconventional meaning in a reading – which invariably fits – and afterwards to check in your favourite Tarot book. You may even decide the book was wrong.

☆ If in doubt look again closely at the cards and person for whom you are reading.

☆ If your mind goes blank as to a meaning or position follow your instinct. Relax. Let your natural intuition flow.

Tarot Courses

Some people attend Tarot courses, either day, weekend or college courses. I myself ran one for a time at a local college. You will see them advertised in New Age magazines or shops. Always make enquiries in advance. If a course is reliable, the tutor will not mind your contacting him or her to ask questions and see whether you feel in tune with them. A tutor or psychic organisation that says that you cannot possibly understand the intricacies of the course in advance or makes you feel inferior should be avoided.

There are no set qualifications in Tarot reading. I have found some well-known clairvoyants who run classes can be intimidating without meaning to and make people feel that their interpretation of the cards is wrong. Clarity, humour, compassion and an ability to listen and learn as well as talk and teach are the qualities you need in a tutor; the grandeur of the surroundings is secondary.

Increasingly colleges of further education and even university departments are offering evening and weekend classes in the psychic arts and do have some control over the quality of the classes.

The whole point of classes is to share skills and expertise: I have found that my own students, even by the second or third week, can show me places where I have been missing the significance of a particular card or spread. Psychic knowledge is not set in stone but evolves – the Tarot is essentially a personal art.

Postal courses are more problematic since the Tarot is essentially an interactive skill. Once you have learned the basics, what you really need is as much practice as possible to widen the context of the cards as they appear in different readings.

Readings for Others

Once you are confident reading for friends and family, you may find it easier to read for strangers, as you know the knowledge is coming for your psyche and you feel less inhibited.

There are many opportunities that arise naturally if you keep your Tarot pack with you; on social occasions, at parties and at work or college. Casually mention your new interest to acquaintances or work colleagues, once you are sure they will not disapprove. Some people get very indignant and call for the exorcists at the first mention of Tarot cards. Before long you will find you are inundated with requests for readings, although some people will wait until you are alone with them to ask. The sceptics are usually the most eager to have a reading.

Go to people's homes or invite them to yours and make

readings at this stage a social occasion.

Do not feel you have to prove anything. Explain that the cards are the focus for a psychic dialogue — that you will suggest meanings and the questioner can apply them. This is not an opt-out. No one would consult a doctor or dentist and expect him or her to guess what was wrong unaided.

Before long you will find that relatives and friends of people for whom you have done readings will ask if you will read for them. Do not read for anyone more than once a week; discourage emotional leeches who demand magical answers, but are totally unwilling to change.

Use the psychic protection described on page 9 then cleanse your cards with your pendulum, especially after encountering negativity. To do this, place your pack face down in a fan. Move your pendulum in anti-clockwise circles five times over the cards to remove any negative feelings, as cards can evoke strong emotions in people as they talk about matters close to their heart. The pendulum will absorb this negativity. When you wash it under running water the energies will flow away, leaving you, the cards and the pendulum refreshed psychically.

At this stage you will probably not want to charge for readings, but accept any gifts with thanks and, if asked about a fee, mention you like flowers or essential oils, or have a charity box in which people can put anonymous donations.

The Next Stage

Once you feel more confident and have confirmation that your readings are accurate, you will naturally relax and may become ready for a greater challenge.

If not, do not feel pressurised. The majority of Tarot

readers do concentrate on friends, family and other interested parties. The problem is usually how to refuse politely if you arrive at a function to find a queue of would-be clients with their problems.

If you do want to test your skills, volunteer to Tarot read for charity at a local fete. This will give you the experience of reading for a large number of people in quick succession and tell you if you would enjoy working as a Tarot reader. I honed my Tarot skills in bookshops while promoting my books and on television and radio doing readings for callers every two or three minutes.

Earning Your Living by the Tarot

The Tarot is such a personal, powerful method that it can be a very exhausting way of earning money if you do it properly. Like a counsellor, psychologist or priest you could come across many life-styles you may not agree with. Unless you are incredibly experienced – and I don't think even a counselling course can prepare you for the intimacy of souls involved in good Tarot readings – you may find that even two in-depth readings are more than you can manage in a day, certainly initially.

However, if you do decide that you do wish to use your gifts professionally, a bonus is that people suddenly start valuing your advice. A Siberian shaman commented that a client should always pay for healing, because otherwise it was not effective. I have discovered that after giving accurate free Tarot readings, strangers, acquaintances and friends alike will often say: 'That was brilliant. Now I will go to a proper Tarot reader (i.e. one who charges) to be sure.'

☆ Begin by charging a moderate amount to a stranger who comes to you via an acquaintance and asks what you charge.

☆ If this feels right, continue to obtain clients by word of mouth. When you are ready advertise in a New Age shop.

☆ Be wary of admitting total strangers to your home if you are alone. If you are a woman, get a man to record a message on your answerphone. Sadly, in this age, advertisements can attract the occasional dubious character.

☆ Arrange appointment times in advance, an hour per person if you are using another form of divination as well, otherwise probably half an hour for an initial appointment. Leave time either side so you can run over if necessary, but establish early on a method of bringing a session to an end or you may end up talking in circles.

☆ Make sure you will not be disturbed and create a calm atmosphere with candles or soft lights, oils and perhaps soft music that helps you both feel relaxed.

☆ Many people who come for readings have a decision to make or are unhappy. Do not be tempted to promise a new love or money to make them happier, but try to steer them to make small plans for step-by-step improvements. Try to limit readings with an individual to once a fortnight or once a week at the most. More frequent sessions can confuse matters and not give time for psychic and earthly efforts to bear fruit.

☆ You are charging for your time and expertise, but cannot and should not be expected to work miracles.

☆ If a client expresses dissatisfaction, help him or her to separate their disappointment with a Tarot message from criticism of your skills. If the client is still being difficult, charge half your normal fee and silently vow never to read for that person again. Some people are professional complainers, who will have visited at least a dozen other clairvoyants in the previous three months and expressed dissatisfaction with them all. They may insist they have a perfect job, the ideal relationship, wonderful children, plenty of money and total happiness, which raises the question of what they want from the reading. Usually doubts will tumble out once you overcome this defensiveness.

☆ At the end of your Tarot sessions, bathe in soothing oils such as lavender, mimosa or ylang-ylang and a psychically cleansing drop or two of pine or eucalyptus.

☆ Before you go to sleep, enclose yourself in a circle of pink light, using an amethyst or rose quartz to protect yourself from excess emotion and negativity, and consciously push your clients' worries out of your mind.

Expanding the Sphere of Work

Once you have a regular clientele and are confident in your abilities, approach a local radio station and offer your services on a late-night show for expenses only in return for mentioning your services.

☆ Book a table at a local psychic fair. Even if you do not make a profit, the experience will be valuable. You can acquire new clients if you take along business cards and flyers.

☆ Look in New Age magazines for forthcoming psychic fairs and approach the organiser. Again ask questions about costs and organisations as some are very spiritual and others merely money-spinners where clairvoyants are forced to cram in too many readings because of the high cost of the tables. If possible, attend one of the fairs as a visitor and talk to the clairvoyants.

☆ The large festivals can book up nine months to a year in advance so contact the organisers very early. Do not be intimidated – the best festivals have friendly organisers who will not demand you sign away rights or insist on stringent conditions. You may also want to offer your services to organise a workshop, perhaps teaching the Tarot.

☆ If you live in a large town a psychic centre or even Spiritualist Church may offer a regular venue in return for a proportion of your takings. Be wary. I know of one psychic centre in London which makes readers sign up for 50 weeks a year and encourages them to persuade clients to return every week. The best centres offer a mutually beneficial and flexible, supportive arrangement.

☆ Finally, never lose sight of the joy and spirituality of your art. You now have a gift and, like all gifts, it flourishes best when used with compassion and humility. Whether you read Tarot cards for yourself or for 30 million people on the most popular TV network in the world, listen to your heart, your soul, your mind. Trust the evidence of your five senses and the all-important sixth sense – call it magic, intuition, psychic awareness, or spirituality. Tune into and share the collective wisdom of the universe which is reflected in and filtered through your Tarot cards.

Appendix

Choosing
a Tarot Pack

Choosing your own Tarot pack is a very special occasion and as such should not be hurried. Try to spend at least half a day. You can buy Tarot cards from large bookshops and department stores as well as New Age outlets. If possible you should buy them personally, rather than through a mail-order outlet, so that you can look through different decks and find the right one for you.

☆ Study the range on offer, but if you do not feel drawn to any of them go elsewhere or return another day. Your Tarot purchase is too important to hurry.

☆ Although most Tarot packs are sealed, there are usually either sample Tarot packs or illustrations of the complete deck on sale.

☆ Try to imagine using each type regularly and for different people. A novel approach may pall or you may find that Vikings or Celts are too specific and you want one of the more general packs that are not tied to one culture.

☆ You need to decide whether you want an illustrated Minor Arcana pack or plain number cards.

☆ Many people do prefer a fully illustrated pack, for example the Rider Waite, the Universal Waite pack or the Mythic Tarot, certainly while learning. Since the Tarot is largely a visual form of divination this may be a valid consideration, so that you are using the same psychic faculties while reading the whole pack.

☆ I would not recommend a Tarot starter pack with the meanings written on individual cards since they may well not be the right meanings for you.

☆ Avoid the more dubious Crowley-inspired witch packs until you are confident that you and you alone are in control.

☆ When you are learning the Tarot, check that your chosen pack does have the standard 22 Major Arcana and 16 Court cards, although they may have different names, for example Shamans and Priestesses, or the names may be in French or Italian.

☆ Beware of packs that don't have any names or numbers. When you are reading it is easy even for an experienced clairvoyant to get confused and you do not want to end up counting Wands or trying to fathom the difference between Justice and Temperance in a dimly lit room.

☆ Make sure that the four suits and 40 Ace to Ten cards also correspond, although the suits may again have different names. If in doubt ask, as some Egyptian or Native North American packs may vary considerably in number and

Tarot

nature, as does the Astrological Tarot. Later you may want to have a variety of packs for different uses.

☆ When you have selected your type of Tarot ask to hold several sealed packs. They do vary and you should choose the one that feels right. If a shop does not allow you time and unobtrusive help, go elsewhere.

☆ Buy a special bag or box for your Tarot. You may want also to purchase a dark silk scarf for wrapping round the pack when not in use.

☆ Afterwards spend some time either in a natural place or among objects of beauty, so that you and the Tarot pack bond in positive circumstances. One pack I bought in a hurry while dashing for a train. I was hot and tired and I never really settled with the cards.

☆ When you get home, even before you make your cards your own with a ritual such as one of those suggested in the Introduction, look at the cards as you would a lovely picture book, letting the images seep into you and find echoes deep within.

Below I have listed a selection of packs that I have found powerful, but this is by no means definitive:

Tarot Decks

The Standard Decks

These are the ones most commonly used by clairvoyants and used to illustrate Tarot books.

The Rider Waite Deck – the most popular deck, based on the Golden Dawn Tradition and beautifully illustrated by Pamela Colman Smith. A very detailed Minor Arcana. Also in mini and large format. You can also get these with the names in French or Spanish.

The Universal Waite Tarot – virtually identical to the original Rider Waite pack. Some people feel that they want to use Waite's cards because it is the original source of this particular design, but since every Tarot pack is unique to its possessor, the Universal deck is, in my view, just as good.

The Aquarian Deck – very similar to the Rider Waite but more sophisticated and to me, less vibrant.

The Marseilles Tarot – with French titles, very stylised and a plain Minor Arcana.

The Classic Deck – similar to the Marseilles, with a plain Minor Arcana, but with more pronounced, almost grotesque images.

The Classic and Marseilles packs may be preferred by those who find the Waite-type packs too flowery.

Fantasy Tarots

The Tarot of the Cat People – for cat lovers. Even the Chariot is pulled by cats!

The Merlin Tarot – a good Tarot if you enjoy fantasy books with dragons and magicians.

Morgain Greer – one of my favourites, has a fairy-tale quality.

Mythological and Symbolic Tarots

The Arthurian Tarot – in search of the Holy Grail. Good for those who love poetic images. The deck has a full-colour Celtic Cross layout sheet.

The Celtic Tarot – features figures from the Celtic tradition, the deities and the myths.

Mythic Astrology Deck – has a beautifully illustrated deck and book set, a good introduction to astrology using the sun, moon, planets and ascendant, but is not a set for learning the basic Tarot.

The Mythic Tarot Deck – a good standard deck for learning with a detailed Minor Arcana. It uses illustrations from Greek and Roman mythology.

The Norse Tarot – depicts Viking warriors and images. For some reason it seems at odds with the Tarot concept, but is quite workable.

Psy-Cards – a 40-card deck is based upon the imagery of archetypes developed by Carl Jung. Each card depicts a concept that evokes subconscious and intuitive impressions within the user. Not strictly a Tarot and so not for learning.

The Motherpeace – large round cards, not for beginners. The suits draw from Native Spiritual traditions and are miniature works of art. They do correspond in many ways to traditional Tarot concepts. They are very difficult to shuffle, but as a second set for an experienced reader, the

Motherpeace deck is one of my favourites. Excellent for meditation.

Historical Tarots

I have also seen reproductions of the early Italian packs which can be large and are usually beautiful and brilliantly coloured.

The Visconti-Sforza Tarrochi Deck – based on an original mid 15th-century pack, this is a beautiful deck, but very large and so difficult to shuffle. The cards do not have names or numbers and can be confusing to interpret for beginners. However, it is a very powerful deck once a reader is more experienced.

The Tarot de Paris – this early 17th-century deck is very beautiful and relatively easy to use, although the titles are in French.

El Gran Tarot Esoterico – my own personal favourite is not strictly historical but a Spanish Romany gypsy pack with a brilliantly coloured Major Arcana that captures the essence of the traditional gypsy world. The names are in Spanish but are relatively easy to follow, although the explanatory leaflet is in Spanish or French. The Minor Arcana is illustrated with simple symbols accompanying the very clear numbering.

Further Reading

Cavendish, Richard, *The Tarot,* Chancellor Press, 1988

Connolly, Eileen, *A New Handbook for the Apprentice,* Aquarian, 1995

Eason, Cassandra, *A Complete Guide to Psychic Development,* Piatkus, 1997

Eason, Cassandra, *Tarot Divination for Today's Woman,* Foulsham, 1994

Eason, Cassandra, *The Complete Guide to Divination,* Piatkus, 1998

Fairfield, Gail, and Provo, Patti, *Inspiration Tarot: A Workbook for Understanding and Creating your own Tarot Deck,* Samuel Weiser, New York, 1991

Fenton, Sasha, *Tarot in Action,* Aquarian, 1991

Freer, Jean, *The New Feminist Tarot,* Aquarian, 1987

Giles, Cynthia, *Tarot: The Complete Guide,* Robert Hale, 1993

Kaplan, Stuart, *The Encyclopaedia of Tarot,* US Games Systems, 1990

Knight, Gareth, *The Magical World of the Tarot,* Aquarian, 1991

Nichols, Sally, *Jung and Tarot: An Archetypal Journey*, Samuel Weiser, New York

Pollack, Rachel, *Seventy-eight Degrees of Wisdom*, Aquarian, 1992

Sargent, Carl, *Personality, Divination and the Tarot*, Destiny Books, 1988

Sharman-Burke, Juliet, *The Complete Book of the Tarot*, Rider, 1991

Waite, A. E., *The Key to the Tarot*, Rider, 1986

Index

Piatkus Guides, written by experts, combine background information with practical exercises, and are designed to change the way you live. Titles include:

Tarot   Cassandra Eason

Tarot's carefully graded advice enables readers to obtain excellent readings from Day One. You will quickly gain a thorough knowledge of both Major and Minor Arcanas and their symbolism, and learn how to use a variety of Tarot spreads.

Meditation   Bill Anderton

Meditation covers the origins, theory and benefits of meditation. It includes over 30 meditations and provides all the advice you need to meditate successfully.

Crystal Wisdom   Andy Baggott and Morningstar

Crystal Wisdom is a fascinating guide to the healing power of crystals. It details the history and most popular modern uses of crystals and vibrational healing. It also covers colour, sound and chakra healing, and gem, crystal and flower essences.

Celtic Wisdom   Andy Baggott

Celtic Wisdom is a dynamic introduction to this popular subject. The author covers Celtic spirituality, the wisdom of trees, animals and stones, ritual and ceremony and much more.

Feng Shui   Jon Sandifer

Feng Shui introduces the origins, theory and practice of the Chinese art of perfect placement, or geomancy. It provides easy-to-follow techniques to help you carry out your own readings and create an auspicious living space.

The Essential Nostradamus   Peter Lemesurier

The Essential Nostradamus charts the life of this extraordinary man, and includes newly discovered facts about his life and work. Peter Lemesurier unravels his prophecies for the coming decades.